Plant Magic

adamsmedia
Adams Media
An Imprint of Simon & Schuster, LLC
100 Technology Center Drive
Stoughton, MA 02072

First published in 2025 by White Star s.r.l.

Vivida

Vivida® is a registered trademark property of White Star s.r.l.
Piazzale Luigi Cadorna, 6
20123 Milan, Italy
www.whitestar.it
Publisher: Balthazar Pagani
Editing and fact checking: Giulia Bilancetti
Translation: Contextus S.r.l., Pavia (Christine Guthry)
Editing: Phillip Gaskill

This Adams Media hardcover edition November 2025

ADAMS MEDIA and colophon are registered trademarks of Simon & Schuster, LLC.

Interior design by Bebung
Illustrations by Quorr

Manufactured in China

10 9 8 7 6 5 4 3 2 1

Library of Congress Cataloging-in-Publication Data has been applied for.

ISBN 978-1-5072-2442-7

Anastasia
Mostacci

Plant Magic

The Magic Connections of Plants with the Universe

Illustrations by
Quorr

Vivida

CONTENTS

ANCESTORS, TEACHERS, ALLIES

When we walk through a forest, in silence and fully aware, among majestic trees and simple shrubs, we can tune in to something invisible yet powerful and real. We realize that we are connected to the whole and can allow ourselves to be nourished by this wonder. When we lie down in a meadow and smell the scent of the damp earth and the plants that inhabit it, when we let ourselves come into contact with the leaves, needles, and barks, or when we taste fruit or smell flowers, we are renewing an ancient association and reaffirming that we belong to the Earth. When we collect and dry herbs, sip an infusion, prepare detoxifying mixtures or a purifying bath, we are mending an ancient relationship that can be re-created and reinvigorated by discovering the value of plants and their magic through daily actions.

We will thus meet teachers, ancestors, allies. We will learn their language, which is non-verbal and addresses the senses and the subtlest perception, involving emotions, thought, and spirit.

The wisdom of plants is revealed in the way they live: their roots are interconnected, they nurture each other, they support each other, they collaborate without competing. They show us how to create community, and simultaneously how to be fully themselves; they bloom and bear fruit at their own pace, perfectly in balance with their surroundings, remaining present through sun, rain, hail, storms, and fire. When a plant dies, it offers itself as nourishment to the others, it's transformed and reborn in the life of its sisters. By accepting and welcoming the flow of life, plants teach us how to embrace the life-death-life cycle, the seasons of the Earth, and our seasons within.

To know the spirit and energy of a plant is to listen and observe it, entering into a relationship with it. It's necessary to open ourselves to the mystery, to be willing to grasp the beauty in what we see—to smell, taste, and feel without the need to explain or control, preserving the mystery in which the wonder resides. We can welcome the unexpected and the different, honor the uniqueness we have before us, and feel connected to the subtle and invisible threads that weave the connections between things, despite our differences.

And so we stand before these green and ancient beings, repositories of our origins and custodians of our future, constantly connected to everything, messengers of the stars and heavenly bodies. We remember that we are part of a sentient cosmos and that, as creatures who appeared on the planet much more recently, we have so much to discover thanks to plants.

Sometimes a relationship with the right plant can do amazing things—catalyzing change, guiding transformation, supporting feelings of grief and pain, or accompanying an evolutionary process, thanks to being filled with wisdom and having experienced, seen, and transformed so much.

Like humans, plants have complex personalities that develop under cosmological influences and by absorbing them. Each planetary force represents a spectrum of potential energy, a particular aspect of the psyche, a fragment of the soul's journey.

Plants, although ancient and pure reflections of the macrocosm, often—just like us—contain mixed planetary influences. Nonetheless, we always recognize a dominant one that governs and expresses itself most prominently.

To become acquainted with a plant, let's approach it with devotion and respect, but above all with curiosity and openness. Let's observe where it grows naturally, what environmental characteristics it prefers. Let's then focus on the shape, the smell, the color, the texture, and the growth cycle. Through the senses, through aromas and flavors, we can grasp how it interacts with our physiology—whether it gives us energy or relaxes us, whether it helps digestion, and on which organs it has the greatest effect.

By considering the energetic aspects, we can then understand whether the plant is warming or refreshing, whether it moistens or dries, and also its psychospiritual properties: how it speaks to our entire system, how it affects the mind and emotions, what it teaches us with its presence, how it shifts energy in our environment.

And thus, little by little, through our relationship with plants, we become able to connect with the fabric of the universe that is inside and outside us. We become aware of a magic composed of relationships, invisible bonds, conspiracies, and cocreations—a magic as old as the world and woven into reality.

Anastasia Mostacci

SUN

The Sun is the source of vitality, the star at the center of our solar system, and the intelligence governing all things. Plants associated with the Sun grow in bright places and are invigorating and warming, and support the heart. On the spiritual plane, they activate in us heat, light, positivity, and expansion.

WATTLE

Acacia (spp.)

The many species of acacia scattered around the world, from the African savannah to the rainforests of Australia, occupy a place of honor in the magic beliefs and practices of many cultures.

In ancient Egypt, this plant—aka Mimosa—was worshipped as a tree of life associated with the goddess Isis. It was considered a symbol of eternal life, so much so that its wood was used to construct coffins. The Babylonians linked it to the goddess Ištar.

In Chinese culture, it's associated with friendship and purity and is used to make incense and perfumes. In Africa, it's regarded as a symbol of resistance and determination, given the fact that the tree even grows in the desert.

It's also said to be a plant capable of promoting spiritual vision and facilitating contact with deities or spirits. Its branches and leaves are the ideal ingredients for ointments and oils that are energizing and promote concentration, while the wood is used to make magic wands due to the wattle's ability to channel and concentrate spiritual energy. Indigenous Australians use wattles for medicinal purposes, as they are useful in healing both physical and spiritual wounds.

The wood can be burned to purify, protect, balance, and—above all—facilitate communication with the invisible world. It is said that planting a wattle tree attracts good luck and prosperity.

The wattle embodies fertility and protection, and its sunny and luminous qualities are considered sacred by the goddess. Let's seek it out to expand these qualities in ourselves.

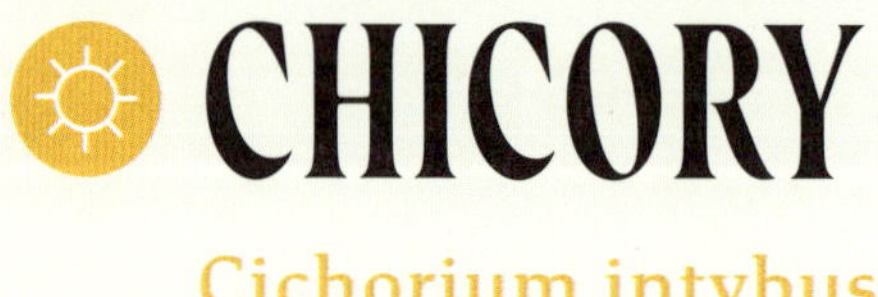

CHICORY

Cichorium intybus

During the sunny hours of the day, chicory's bright blue flowers skirt the roadside, but they shut after sunset or on cloudy days, leaving visible only the hollow, rough stems covered in light down.

Chicory blooms for a single day, and is always facing the light—that's why it is also known as "the bride of the sun." In pre-Celtic times, it was a highly revered, sacred plant, considered the incarnation of the goddess of vegetation, daughter of Mother Earth, who with her blue eyes constantly looked at the Sun god, her husband.

It's a symbol of devoted love, often linked to vain expectations, but also to hope. Its magic properties are connected to protection and invisibility.

It was believed that the flowers could facilitate childbirth and, when mixed with food, prevent love from going astray. Shamans use chicory to speed up and slow down time while walking. In fact, it's sometimes called the "clock flower" precisely because of its link to the Sun and the passing of time.

Roasting the roots makes a viable coffee substitute that was very popular in the second half of the nineteenth century to dilute the real drink, which was was very expensive at that time. The leaves, which have a bitter taste, contain vitamin C and inulin and can be eaten in salads. It has diuretic properties, detoxifies the liver, and tones the digestive system.

Chicory helps us see the truth clearly and free ourselves from illusion, allowing us to bring into the light of day all that needs to be seen and heard.

LEMON

Citrus limon

With its yellow fruit symbolizing positive energy, abundance, and prosperity, lemon radiates solar strength and purity.

Although closely associated with the Mediterranean, it is believed that the lemon is native to Asia, more likely India, though nowadays it's grown in all tropical and subtropical regions of the globe. It is a hybrid between bitter orange and cedar; in fact, its name derives from the Persian word *līmūn*, which refers to citrus fruit in general.

The ancient Egyptians used it for both culinary and medicinal purposes, while in the Middle Ages it was introduced to Europe as a luxury good and a symbol of wealth, often offered as a gift to royalty. In medicine, lemons have been used to combat sore throats and respiratory tract infections, while the juice and peel were believed to promote digestion.

Its magical uses are associated with purification, repelling evil, and evoking prosperity, especially thanks to the flowers, which are common ingredients in rituals of love and attraction.

Adding lemon juice when washing floors, doors, and windows helps remove stagnant, heavy energy. We can also use it in a cleansing bath to manage negativity and a busy mind. We can place lemons on the threshold and inside the house for protection—if they dry out without turning moldy, the environment is healthy; otherwise, it indicates the presence of heavy energy.

Purifying, uplifting, vibrant: lemon's aroma renews us by connecting us to our highest potential and allowing us to attract opportunities and good luck.

SAFFRON CROCUS

Crocus sativus

Its beautiful flowers, like small cups, welcome the sun's rays, revealing thin golden threads, precious and aromatic inside.

Long a symbol of material and spiritual wealth, joy, prosperity, life, light, and warmth, saffron has been a renowned dyeing plant used to capture the Sun's golden yellow hue since ancient times. It's been called upon to dye the clothes of Assyrian kings, the bandages of Egyptian mummies, and the veils of ancient Roman brides, but also to prepare food, wines, ointments, and medicines.

The Greek myth recounting its origins tells of the young Krokos, who was transformed into a saffron crocus out of revenge after he'd fallen in love with the nymph Smyrna, who was, in turn, loved by the god Hermes.

It's a tonic for the mind and body that can be used to reduce pain, treat infections, stimulate the heart rate, and activate metabolism and digestion. Associated with vitality and fertility, it's also known as an aphrodisiac and is given to newlyweds, or placed in newborns' cribs for healthy growth.

In fact, its protective qualities can be used in amulets and talismans. It can be of great support in times of loss and mourning, low vital energy, and postpartum. We may ingest it in food and drink to integrate its warming, aromatic, and vitalizing qualities.

Let's seek out this plant of the Sun to fortify our hearts and be flooded by its radiant warmth, to elevate our spirits and nurture our inner light by dispelling the darkness.

BAY TREE

Laurus nobilis

This aromatic shrub is known for its countless beneficial properties concentrated in the leaves and berries, which release an unmistakable aroma.

Bay tree's scientific name is composed of the Latin words *Laurus*, which means "verdant," and *nobilis*, which means "noble" or "of high rank." In fact, the plant is associated with honor and glory. In ancient Greece and Rome, the practice of crowning important men and women—such as kings, heroes, athletes, and poets—with a laurel wreath to state their greatness was widespread.

Always considered a symbol of wisdom and knowledge, it was linked to the Greek god Apollo, guardian of intellect and inspiration. According to the myth, the god of the Sun fell madly in love with the nymph Daphne, who, to escape him, asked her father Peneus for help. The nymph thus was transformed into a bay tree, and Apollo expressed his love by making the bay tree his sacred plant, wearing it on his head and growing it in all his temples.

It's said that the high priestess, the Oracle of Delphi, chewed on its leaves and inhaled its smoke to promote visions and divinations. In common lore, shredded leaves hidden under the pillow can promote clairvoyant dreams, while laurel wreaths are believed to be effective for protection and conferring courage to the wearer.

Bay also aids digestion, stimulates metabolism and diuresis, supports the immune system, and improves concentration.

Let's select it to celebrate our worth, enjoy the fruits of our labor, reward our efforts, and shower ourselves in the golden light of success and fulfillment.

OLIVE TREE

Olea europaea

A symbol of the Mediterranean, this is a long-lived and life-sustaining tree with a silvery appearance and fruits that conceal the golden, valuable oil inside.

It's said that the first olive seed came from the earthly paradise, and an olive branch is what the dove announcing the end of the floods to Noah carried in its beak. A Greek myth links the olive tree to Athena, the goddess of wisdom—who, in a competition with Poseidon, the god of the sea, gifted the plant to the city of Athens, which has since taken her name.

The olive tree is an eternal plant, capable of surviving for centuries, reaching a height of almost 50 feet (15 meters). Eating its fruits and oil is a way to ensure a long and healthy life, thanks to its excellent content of healthy fats and their widely recognized beneficial properties. By virtue of its longevity, it was used in the bouquets of ancient wedding rites, and the spouses were then invited to plant a sapling. Famously, Ulysses' bedroom in Ithaca was dug from the trunk of a large olive tree.

The tree is central to Christian worship as well: its blessed oil is used to celebrate baptisms, confirmations, and last rites. Even in the Koran, its oil symbolizes the light of god, which if placed in a crystal ampoule illuminates like a sparkling star.

Let us seek it out to move toward the light, so that we may become a beacon for those around us, to sense and share with our loved ones the splendor of our soul.

ROSEMARY

Rosmarinus officinalis

With its indigo flowers and narrow leaves—but above all, its wonderful scent—this shrub embodies the essence of the Mediterranean.

Growing in arid and sandy soils from coastal areas to highlands, rosemary is used extensively as an aromatic in cooking, as well as for its healing, antimicrobial, energizing, purifying, and magical properties.

Its name derives from the Latin *Ros marinus*, or "dew of the sea." It evokes the radiant, heavenly force, combined with the power of water that, in meeting, flood and enliven the Earth and its plants. It provides a real boost of energy, promotes microcirculation, supports the memory, tones the heart, and strengthens the bones.

The Egyptians used its twigs to embalm the dead, while the ancient Greeks and Romans burned them for purification prior to a banquet, ritual, or festival, and as an offering to please the gods. Traditionally, it was used at weddings to symbolize marital fidelity and promote fertility. It was also placed on the cradle to protect the newborn, under the bed to ward off negativity and nightmares, and in hospital rooms to purify the space and promote healing.

Planting a rosemary bush at the entrance of a home drives away negative people and thieves. Added to the bathwater, it provides lasting positive energy and strength, making us memorable to the eyes of those around us.

Like a sea breeze, rosemary caresses us, awakening body, mind, and spirit, while its solar energy helps us shine increasingly more.

ASHWAGANDHA

Withania somnifera

Also called "Indian ginseng" or "winter cherry," this woody evergreen shrub bears fruit ranging from yellow to bright red.

In Sanskrit, "ashwagandha" means "smell of horse" and refers to its ability to bestow the strength and stamina of this animal. The botanical term *somnifera* refers to its relaxing and regenerating properties.

It belongs to the Solanaceae family, native to the Mediterranean basin, East Africa, and Southwest Asia, and it has been used in traditional Indian medicine for over 4,000 years.

In Hindu mythology, it's associated with the god Shiva, who is believed to have used the herb to increase his strength and vitality. For this reason, it's also used in spiritual practices to promote meditation and relaxation. It has a calming and grounding effect on the mind and body, bringing peace, clarity, and a sense of inner brightness and radiance.

It's one of the most important adaptogenic plants in the world, appreciated by people of all ages. It's capable of improving reproductive function in both men and women, as well as counteracting inflammation, repairing the nervous system, and facilitating adrenal recovery, reversing the damage of aging and promoting longevity. The benefit of adaptogenic plants is precisely this: to provide the body and mind with what they need, restoring balance.

Ashwagandha's restorative and revitalizing energy meets us where we are, nurturing our needs and making us lighter and brighter.

GINGER

Zingiber officinalis

Known for its warming properties, ginger was considered a sacred root by many ancient cultures.

A native plant of Asia, ginger is related to turmeric, galangal, and cardamom. In Asian lore, it was believed to ward off evil spirits and protect against bad luck, and it was a common offering in rituals invoking strength, protection, and prosperity.

In medieval Europe, ginger was prized for its ability to cure a variety of ailments, and was often used in potions to increase vitality and prevent disease. It was one of the first spices traded along the Eastern routes and the Silk Road. The English settlers and Spanish conquistadors spread it to North and South America, the South Pacific, and the Caribbean.

It has the capability to ignite fire, both digestive and erotic; it also injects passion into relationships, ignites courage, instills confidence, and speeds up processes. It is said that a piece of ginger under the bed puts an end to nightmares and provides a sense of safety and protection. If worn, it has the effect of an energy shield and also protects travelers.

It can be added to the bathwater or herbal teas to purify the body and spirit, favoring renewal and positive energy flows. On a magical level, it should be considered a catalyst for success and prosperity.

Ruled by the Sun, this spice ignites in us fire's best qualities: direction, clarity, elevation, warmth, passion, and manifestation.

We collect solar plants on Sundays, a day in which we can also devote ourselves to health, personal growth, play, and being with others. To realign ourselves with the life force, we can start the day by drinking hot lemon water; taking an invigorating bath with laurel, rosemary, and ginger; and nourishing ourselves on a deep level by integrating the products of the olive tree, saffron, and ashwagandha.

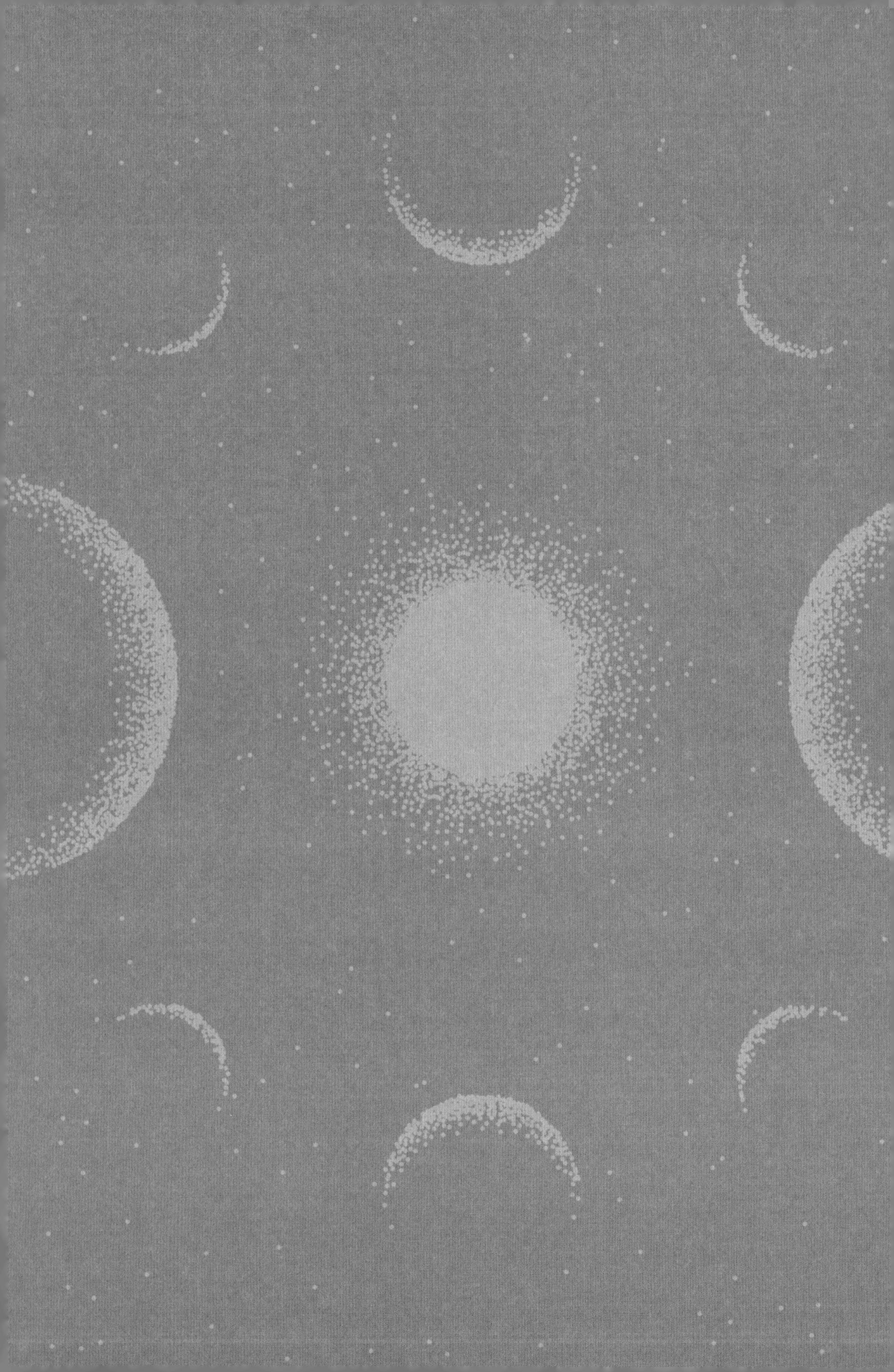

MOON

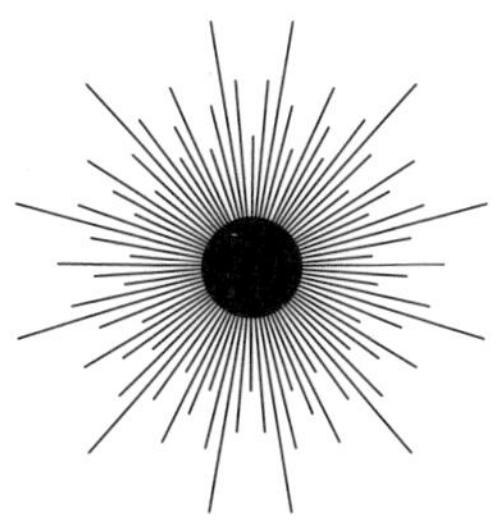

The Moon is queen of the waters, linked to tides, birth, and emotions. Symbolizing the natural cycles, it embodies the beginning and end of all things, the night, changeability, childhood, and imagination. The Moon is soft, full, and bright, but also dark and mysterious. Lunar plants are nutritious, moist, and juicy; they affect fluids, the lymph, stomach, brain, and female organs.

MUGWORT

Artemisia vulgaris

This is the lunar plant par excellence, linked to the cyclical feminine. Its leaves reveal a concealed silvery side that speaks to mystery, the unconscious, the magic that we may find on the road, an apparition as common as it is powerful.

Indigenous to Asia and North America, widespread throughout the northern hemisphere, mugwort grows with great resilience in ditches, fields, and uncultivated lands.

Its scientific name derives from the Greek goddess Artemis, goddess of hunting and the Moon, protector of women and children, guardian of untouched wilderness and the untouched feminine.

It is a plant that prompts us to reconnect with our instincts and intuition. It is connected to an underground forest that inhabits us, to secret emotional sources, to deep inner wisdom that demands to be revealed and recalled. It is profoundly uterine, and it invites a descent toward our interior world and authenticity, recirculating what is blocked, stagnant, and must be released. It acts on the production of oxytocin, the love hormone that is secreted during childbirth, sexuality, touching, and moments of well-being when we bond and connect deeply.

Considered the plant of witches and healers, it can be used as an herbal tea, burned for purification, or kept under the pillow to promote dreams.

Mugwort is wise; it promotes memory and protects us. It can lead us on a path of plant spirits, opening doors and bestowing vision, amplifying our extrasensory perception. Let us seek it out to integrate our shadows, embrace our neglected parts, and open ourselves to welcome all the magic of the wild soul.

GUM TREE

Eucalyptus

In its leaves we find the Moon: the young ones are round, tender, and silvery; the mature ones are dark green and shaped like a sickle.

This is a majestic evergreen tree of the *Myrtaceae* family. Native to Australia, Papua New Guinea, Indonesia, and the Philippines, it's now widespread across the world, encompassing over 600 species.

Aboriginal peoples use it for healing wounds, speeding up healing, and preventing infections. With its trunk hollowed by termites, then suitably cleaned out and decorated with traditional motifs, they craft the didgeridoo, and this "sound stick" is a sacred instrument to indigenous Australians. In Aboriginal culture, the gum tree is a cultural symbol that for some groups represents a guardian spirit. The leaves of some gum trees are the main source of nutrition for koalas.

Most smooth-bark gum trees shed their bark, with the ash-gray layer giving way to a reddish wood. The roots are long and absorb a lot of water, making it a precious ally in restoring damaged land. Its balsamic scent purifies the air and invigorates body and mind.

Associated with Selene, the Greek goddess of the Moon, often depicted on her chariot as she lights up the night sky, this is a female plant that carries the intense elemental energies of water and air. In the practice of magic, it is used for cleansing, protection, and healing; it is said that carrying a gum leaf in your pocket or shoe protects against adverse situations, and that burning it instantly dispels negative energy and attracts positive vibrations.

Gum tree purifies our communication like a fresh lunar balm, connecting us with our inner waters.

PINK IPÊ

Handroanthus impetiginosus

Its timber vibrates with the black Moon (the second occurrence of a New Moon in a month) and embodies the archetype of the dark goddess. Like a cosmic womb, it is capable of gestating and birthing what is not yet known, yet is alive in us, allowing it to emerge and express itself.

This majestic tree, native to the Amazon rainforest, is over 65 feet (20 meters) tall, has intense pink flowers and a dark, hard, and crackled bark that grows back quickly without compromising the tree's health when it's removed.

In fact, the inner part of the bark has been used for medical purposes for centuries by tribes throughout Central and South America. Shamans used it as a tonic, an aphrodisiac, and a stimulant, and at times it was added to the psychoactive beverage ayahuasca.

It was used in ancient times to make hunting bows and other magical tools, since it was loaded with strength and resilience. Native peoples used it as a panacea, and since the 1980s the pink ipê has been the subject of scientific studies due to its anti-inflammatory, antimicrobial, cancer-preventing, and antifungal properties. It is also able to assist with menstrual issues and the immune system. Thanks to its lunar qualities, it can improve psychic abilities, divination, and dream work, and guard against negative energy.

We can turn to it during healing rituals and to enhance the magic power of other plants and medicines. In addition, we can drink its tea, use its bark immersed in water for bathing, or burn it to cleanse ourselves and a space.

The pink ipê is plant protector of the sacred, of the deep regeneration that takes place in the dark and allows us to shine. It knows how to reconnect us with our inner selves, dispel our fear of the unknown, and guide us in how to connect to the splendor of our hidden potential.

WILD LETTUCE

Lactuca virosa

A relative of the more common garden lettuce, it stands out for its tall, elegant stem and milky white sap, and it has a rich history of traditional uses.

Wild lettuce originally grew in much of Central Europe, North Africa, and Western Asia. During colonization, it was introduced to North America and Australia.

In ancient Egypt, it was associated with Min, a deity of fertility comparable to the vigorous Pan, the deity whose statue, surrounded by wild lettuce, was carried in processions during the festivals devoted to him. The Egyptians used the plant as an aphrodisiac, while the Greeks used it as an anaphrodisiac: it was part of the diet of priests. Due to the white latex it produces, it was employed to treat sexual problems such as premature ejaculation and nocturnal emissions. It can be used in fertility rituals or added to love potions.

Hippocrates prescribed the plant for its sedative and healing properties. The Roman emperor Augustus, who successfully used it to overcome a serious illness, dedicated a large statue to the physician who put him on a lettuce diet. Augustus disseminated the plant all over the world as a cure. Its sedative properties continued to be appreciated in the nineteenth century, so much so that it was referred to as "the poor man's opium." It was also used to calm restless children, soothe coughs, and promote sleep.

Wild lettuce can be used in a magical bath to promote a sense of calm and relaxation; it can be kept in a medicine pouch under the pillow to foster peaceful and loving dreams; and it can be incorporated into meditation or burned like incense to amplify the powers of divination.

Connected to the Moon's soft gentleness, this plant has a calming and magical influence capable of promoting love, peace, and connection.

SPIKENARD

Nardostachys jatamansi

Its name comes from the Semitic root "NR," which means to shine or illuminate with reflected light, just like the Moon does.

Spikenard is a plant with small pink bell-shaped flowers gathered in a sphere at the top of the stem. It belongs to the *Caprifoliaceae* family and grows in the eastern Himalayas at elevations of about 10,00–16,000 feet (3,000–5,000 meters). Today it is at risk of extinction due to overexploitation, intensive grazing, and the progressive deterioration of its habitat.

The term *jatamansi* in Sanskrit means "gray hair" and refers to the plant's ability to promote longevity and vitality. According to tradition, its rhizomes were offered to the Buddha at the moment of enlightenment. It is mentioned in the Ayurvedic scriptures, where its balancing properties on the mind and emotions are valued. It is also mentioned in the Bible, where it appears as a symbol of devotion and is used for anointing. The intensely aromatic essential oil that is extracted from the crushed and distilled rhizomes is used as a perfume, as a traditional medicine, and in religious ceremonies.

Associated with love and healing and revered for its protective and purifying properties, spikenard has been used in cleansing rituals, in blessings, and for spiritual growth, as well as in rituals to attract true love, improve psychic abilities, and deepen meditation.

It can be burned like incense, added to a cleansing bath, carried like a talisman. Above all, we can use it to anoint ourselves and devotedly connect with life's mysteries. It's ideal for women celebrating menstrual days linked to the New Moon.

This plant's lunar energy connects us to our roots and elevates our hearts, expanding love and transforming it in service to life.

WILLOW

Salix (spp.)

Trees belonging to the Salix genus are the lunar plants par excellence. With their silvery leaves resembling a crescent moon, they are linked to the feminine, water, and emotions.

Native to Europe, Asia, and North America, willow is easily recognized for its dense foliage and branches that in some species cascade toward the ground.

The name originates from a Celtic language and means "near water," and it's indeed often found on the banks of rivers or lakes and in places rich in water resources. When it doesn't find surface water, it seeks it in the depths of the Earth. It grows quickly and can live up to 100 years. It also knows how to rise again—when it falls, the branches touching the damp soil immediately take root, giving life to new trees. Thus, it teaches us that regeneration and rebirth are always possible, starting from the water, meaning the realm of perception and emotion.

In Celtic mythology, the willow was sacred to Brigid, the goddess of fertility who represents the promise of spring and is the protector of poets, artists, healers, and druids. Furthermore, it was considered home to elves, fairies, and goblins. Women and healers turned to this tree seeking to connect with the invisible world; with magic and prophecy. During the European witch hunts, any woman standing next to a willow tree risked being accused of witchcraft and burned at the stake.

The first evidence of its use is found on a 3,000-year-old Babylonian tablet. Later, Hippocrates attested to its efficacy in relieving fever and pain. Its properties are: antipyretic, analgesic, anti-inflammatory, antirheumatic, sedative, and anti-anemia. It also supports the hormonal system and female and menstrual physiology.

Willow teaches us to let things flow, to regenerate and be a fertile soil, to take care of what is emerging and sprouting within us.

SANDALWOOD

Santalum album

The fragrance of this wood, which is present in almost every Indian home and temple, is unmistakable and enveloping—and it calls us to reconnect with the sacred.

Its scientific name derives from Sanskrit and means "bright white," referring to the tree's light-colored wood. Native to India, Sri Lanka, and Indonesia, it's now at risk of extinction because it's so sought-after. The tree can reach up to 33 feet (10 meters) in height. It's considered a semi-parasitic plant, as it often seeks the shade of other trees and draws nourishment from their roots. The more arid and barren the soil into which it sinks its roots, the more intense its scent is.

The Vedas, the ancient Indian texts dating back to the fifth century BCE, mentioned sandalwood, which was sacred to the god Shiva. Its wood was used to build temples and statues of deities. Due to its ability to withstand termite attacks, it has always been considered a tree capable of providing protection. It is also said to neutralize the venom of scorpions and snakes. In India, sandalwood powder is sprinkled on the funeral pyres of wealthy and prominent citizens to promote a better reincarnation.

It is used in yoga and tantric practice so that its aroma will awaken the Kundalini snake, encouraging the basic sexual energy to rise toward the expanded consciousness of the cosmos and open the third eye. It's considered an aphrodisiac capable of connecting sexuality with a calming and meditative dimension.

Sandalwood is anti-inflammatory, soothing, and refreshing to the skin. Precisely because of its very high vibration, it is believed to be able to ward off evil spirits and negative energy. It can even make wishes come true if a person writes them on a piece of wood, then confidently burns it.

Let's seek out sandalwood for its calming and refreshing qualities that brighten and balance the mind and the emotional waters, and for its vibration, which is a soothing lunar nectar.

CHASTEBERRY

Vitex agnus castus

With its spikes of flowers ranging from purple to lilac and white and its peppercorn-like fruit reminiscent of small black moons, this plant evokes a calming and healing energy capable of heightening our receptive nature.

Also known as "monks' pepper," the chasteberry is a shrub belonging to the *Verbenaceae* family, widespread in Central Asia and various Mediterranean regions.

Its name refers to purity and chastity, reminding us that it was traditionally credited with the ability to appease the libido. Pliny the Elder stated that it was sprinkled over the beds of Athenian women to keep them faithful while their husbands were at war. It was associated with the goddess Hera, protector of marriage, and with Demeter, goddess of harvest and fertility, whose temples were decorated with flowering branches of chasteberry during the festivities dedicated to her. Even in ancient times, its soothing properties on the female hormonal cycle were known and it was employed for issues relating to gynecological health and fertility. In the Middle Ages, the plant was grown in monks' gardens and the seeds taken as an anaphrodisiac decoction to help the monks uphold their vows of chastity.

The chasteberry is also known as "Vencedor," meaning "victorious," and can be used in ritual baths to help overcome challenges and succeed in the world. It is also considered a sacred plant for cleansing the energy of the home and to aid our emotional purification.

The lunar energy of chasteberry is like a nectar that restores balance by calming excesses and evening out imbalances, fostering fertility (understood as living harmony from which everything flows), and healing our shadows and what is jarring with the sweet tonic of temperance.

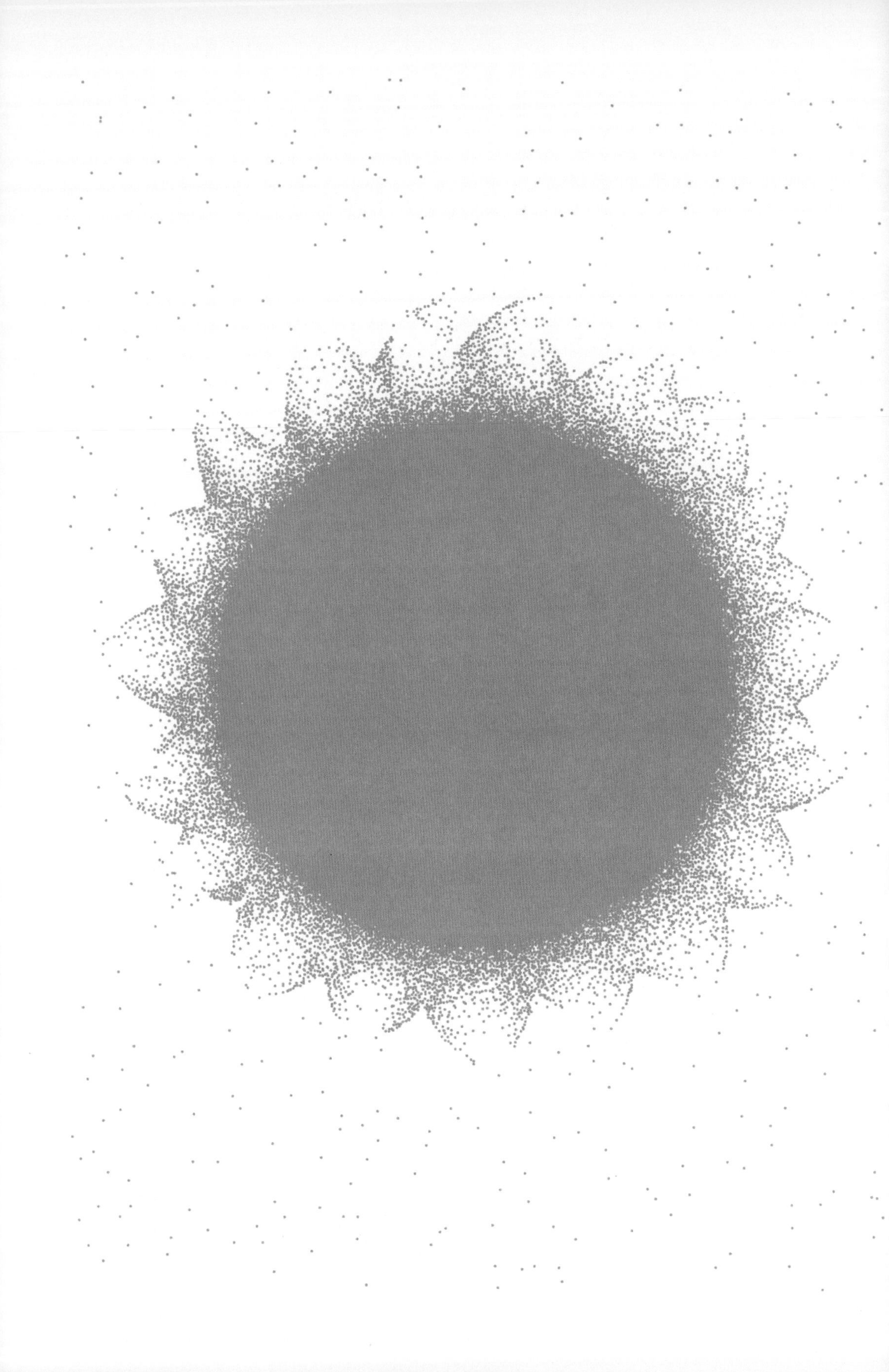

Mondays, we can pick lunar plants and engage in creative, meditative, and water-related activities. Let's rest under a willow tree, burn some sandalwood to ease the mind, and, after a nice bath with eucalyptus leaves, massage ourselves with spikenard oil. We can sip a cup of mugwort before bed to facilitate connecting with our dreams and the flowing of emotions.

MARS

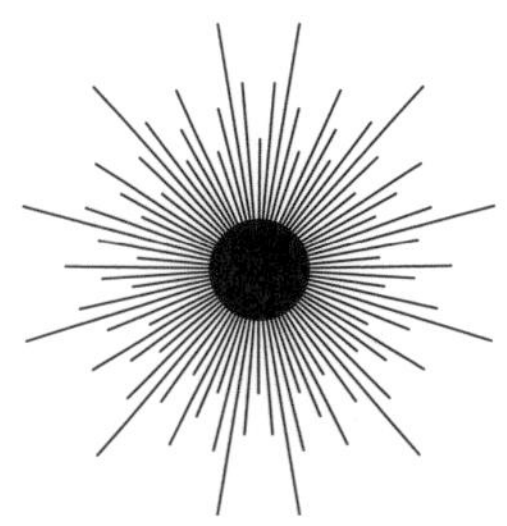

Mars represents the warrior god, the active force, and courage. Its element is fire, the energy of action. It is the servant of the Sun, putting its vigor at the service of the heart and defending it. When unfocused, it risks being emotionally overwhelmed by anger and being defined by briskness, eruptions, and impulsivity. Plants associated with Mars are often thorny and sharp, and they exhibit intensely defensive and stimulating actions.

GARLIC

Allium Sativum

This bulbous plant with a high stem is loved as much in the kitchen (for its spicy flavor) as it is feared for its strong and sulfurous smell, which persists long after it has been consumed.

Of Asian origin, but now widespread all over the world, the name *allium* is linked to an ancient Celtic word, *all*, which means "monster-slayer" and is used in many traditions to ward off evil spirits. It's also considered a plant connected to the afterlife.

Cloves of garlic have been found among Egyptian graves and in the enclosures of sacred animals in the Saqqara necropolis. In fact, garlic was widely used in ancient Egypt, as some inscriptions on the pyramids confirm, attesting to what the workers ate during the construction. Hippocrates and Dioscorides, the most prominent Greek doctors, also used it to treat skin lesions, digestive disorders, intestinal infections, and heart failure. Its active ingredient encourages the control of cholesterol and triglycerides, improving metabolic wellness.

In European folklore, garlic has always been considered a powerful amulet against the evil eye. Wearing a bag of fresh cloves or hanging a braid of bulbs at the head of the bed or on the door is considered an effective safeguard against vampires, werewolves, and demons.

In addition to being a powerful antiparasitic and dewormer, garlic has the ability to ward off people, situations, or personality traits that rob our energy, time, emotions, and money, violating our life energy.

Its spicy heat activates inner cleansing: it's like a flame that burns everything that is harmful or excessive, like a warrior with a shining sword, decapitating all that is harmful inside and outside us.

♂ CAYENNE PEPPER

Capsicum annuum

With its flame-shaped red fruit—spicy on the tongue and capable of warming to the point of making you sweat—this is a plant that embodies fire and knows how to ignite life.

Cayenne pepper has a long history, dating back thousands of years in Central and South America. It was grown by native populations for both culinary and medicinal purposes, mainly to relieve stomach ailments, cramps, and bloating, and to support the circulatory system. In fact, it has the ability to invigorate the digestive system, extract toxins from tissue, and relieve joint and muscle pains.

Later, in the fifteenth and sixteenth centuries, this ancient variety of pre-Columbian origin spread all over the world thanks to Portuguese seafarers and traders. The name "Cayenne" derives from the city Cayenne, the capital of French Guiana, while the scientific name dates back to the Latin *capsa*, meaning "box" (referencing the particular shape of its fruit, which resembles a container with seeds inside).

In spiritual practice, it's used to seek visions, amplify the effect of other herbs, and accelerate the manifestation of spells. It is an integral part of purification rituals and can be sprinkled in specific areas of the house for spiritual protection. Tying the peppers in a wreath and hanging them on the door of the house will attract positive energy.

Thanks to its energizing effects on the body, it promotes heightened spiritual awareness and, by virtue of its balancing action on the heart, can lend enthusiasm to romantic relationships or help overcome a breakup.

Its fire is vibrant and its pulsating medicine supports vitality in its highest expression, helping us light up and dance like bright flames.

TOBACCO

Nicotiana tabacum

This is one of the most widely used plants for recreational purposes, and its improper use causes addiction. Indigenous peoples, however, consider it a master plant, honoring it with the nickname "grandfather" and venerating it with respect and devotion.

Native to Brazil, Uruguay, Paraguay, and Argentina, tobacco's presence was fairly extensive in large parts of the tropical forests of the Andes and the Caribbean, becoming an integral part of the ritualistic practices of South and Central American tribes.

Christopher Columbus's sailors were amazed to discover the indigenous peoples' habit of smoking tobacco, so much so that they mocked them by nicknaming them "chimneys." The Arabic word *tabaq,* meaning "euphoria-producing herb," may explain the origin of the name, while the term *Nicotiana* is attributed to Jean Nicot, who first introduced the plant to the French court in 1550.

According to Native American tradition, the Great Spirit gave each creature a special power; and, since there were no powers left when he created humans, he gave them tobacco, so they could safeguard it, trade it, and use it to conjure the spirits. That is why it's offered during spiritual and ceremonial practices and shared to sanction alliances and contracts, friendships, and the beginnings of journeys and wars.

Smoking can be used to purify and cleanse spaces, objects, and people, and to facilitate communication with ancestors or the deceased. It's also used as *rapè*, a mixture of dried and pulverized plants that is blown directly into the nostrils to progressively clear the perceptual and extraperceptual channels.

Its effect on the central nervous system makes it an activating, strongly purifying, and revitalizing medicine that is linked to wisdom, vision, and connecting with the Spirit.

BLACKTHORN

Prunus spinosa

Belonging to the Rosaceae (rose) family—with its beautiful flowers announcing spring and its large, dark, pointed thorns—this shrub speaks to light and shadow.

Related to the hawthorn, blackthorn grows in Europe, Asia, and North Africa, forming impenetrable shrubbery that acts as a refuge for birds and other wildlife. Its long black thorns can cause wounds that are easily infected. The bark, flowers, and leaves contain a toxic substance that over time has caused many deaths, leading to its being associated with witches, the devil, and the dark goddess. At the same time, its bright white flowers make it a bright plant linked to fertility and the celebration of Beltane. Its ripe berries can be safely eaten, and they are very rich in vitamin C.

In Irish folklore, the blackthorn is protected by a fairy tribe, the Lunantisidhe—small, sharp, and angry creatures who are said to curse those who try to cut down the tree during Samhain.

There are many magical uses that relate to protection, including: hanging a branch collected during the full moon on a front door; carrying dried berries and thorns in a small bag; and burning wood in purification ceremonies, specifically during the winter solstice to celebrate the return of the sun.

Its Mars-driven force acts on all our potential—strengthening the cardiac and circulatory systems, helping us overcome adversity, increasing awareness of the energy surrounding us, and supporting us as a fierce protector.

Blackthorn supports our need to go inward and see the shadowy aspects by learning to welcome them; it teaches us to embrace darkness as much as light, because they are two inseparable parts of nature, including our own.

BLACK LOCUST

Robinia pseudoacacia

This is a thorny tree that emerges bare and skeletal from the earth, covering itself in green foliage and clusters of scented white flowers in late spring.

The black locust hails from the Appalachian Mountains in North America, where it's part of Appalachia's mixed mesophytic forests.

The great naturalist Carl Linnaeus named it in honor of Jean Robin, the pharmacist to Henry IV, the king of France who germinated the seeds in the Botanical Garden of Paris in 1601.

It's a tree that helps regenerate damaged ecosystems: as other plants grow and the ecological succession continues, it dies to give way to other species. Its wood has been widely used because it can last 100 years without deteriorating. Native Americans used it to make bows, and it was one of the first construction materials to be exported. The Cherokee people chewed the root bark to induce vomiting and relieve toothaches, while it was believed that a flower-based tea could cure everything from headaches to nausea.

It's used in spells for personal protection and power: the dry resin and leaves can be burned over charcoal to nurture a feeling of inner dominion and to increase psychic powers. It's a melliferous plant that produces a delicately flavored honey. Its flowers are delicious in infusions and pancakes, while the other parts of the plant are toxic and must be handled with care.

With its pointy thorns and alkaloid content, the black locust expresses the power of Mars. It invites us to see how, in welcoming and embracing the shadows cautiously and fearlessly, we can tap into the sweetest and most nutritious aspects of coming into bloom.

♂ BUTCHER'S BROOM

Ruscus aculeatus

The pointed leaves and red berries make this a traditional decorative element during the Christmas holidays, and clearly show that it belongs to the warm, warrior energy of Mars.

Butcher's broom is an evergreen shrub from the *Asparagaceae* family. It grows about 12–31 inches (30–80 centimeters) tall, and is native to Eurasia, though it's also found in Mediterranean and Atlantic areas.

The Italian name, *pungitopo* (mouse stinger), stems from the peasant custom of placing it in pantries to protect food from mice. In English, however, its name refers to its twigs being used to clear the counters and blocks in butcher's shops.

The Germanic people considered it a good-luck charm capable of warding off evil spirits, and they protected their homes by planting it around the property. This tradition also reached the Romans. The Latins exchanged butcher's broom sprigs as a good omen, while for the Christians it symbolized fertility. Its red berries color the winter during the solstice, reminding us that the sun will return to shine and warm us, putting an end to the harsh winter.

It's a protective plant with anti-inflammatory, diuretic, and antirheumatic properties. It affects the blood circulation and menstrual flow, and is used as a vasoconstrictor. In addition, its roasted seeds were used as a substitute for coffee, a root decoction was recommended to eliminate gallstones or heal broken bones, and its bitter-tasting sprouts are delicious and can be cooked like asparagus.

Burning the roots as incense brings calm and promotes divination and presence, although the entire plant can be used in spells and energetic cleansing.

Let's choose this little warrior for its strength, protection, and readiness to defend and nurture the light. It safeguards borders so there may be no dispersions or invasions.

CLOVE

Syzygium aromaticum

The small, aromatic buds of this plant represent much more than a spice with a pungent aroma; they are powerful, life-affirming beings that make it vibrant and stimulating.

This evergreen tree, belonging to the *Myrtaceae* family, grows to 33–49 feet (10–15 meters) tall, and is native to Indonesia but is widespread throughout the East. It produces small buds rich in essential oil, and is appreciated as a spice all over the world.

Cloves arrived in the West via the caravan routes, although the ancient Romans were already using them for their antiseptic properties and for soothing tooth pain. Cloves were also found in the tombs of the pharaohs, added as an aromatic offering to accompany the deceased on their journeys into the afterlife, while their pungent scent also served as an embalming agent. They also played a central role in ceremonies invoking divine favors or to ensure an abundant harvest.

In the Chinese tradition, it was common practice to chew a clove before meeting the emperor. It was meant both as a gesture of respect and as an offer of good will and positive energy, due to its stimulating effects on energy flow and vitality. In Europe, during the Middle Ages, cloves were associated with protection against the evil eye and were woven into garlands to keep malevolent forces at bay.

Hanging cloves at home—perhaps stuck inside an orange like a pomander—purifies the rooms and creates an energy shield; the same effect can be achieved by wearing them. Chewing them promotes vitality and fuels spiritual resilience, connecting us to cosmic powers. They're also considered powerful amulets for attracting love and abundance into one's life.

Let us seek out cloves to revitalize and stimulate our mental and physical energies, and to invoke courage, inner strength, health, and protection.

CAT'S CLAW

Uncaria tomentosa

Considered a miracle plant originating from the depths of the Amazon rainforest, cat's claw is a woody vine that can reach 98 feet (30 meters) in height!

Cat's claw grows in Peru, Colombia, and Bolivia at an altitude between 328 and 1,640 feet (100–500 meters), and gets its name from the small, claw-like thorns on its stem. The bark and root are made into liquid extracts, capsules, tablets, and herbal teas that contain the plant's therapeutic powers.

It has long been used as a traditional medicine by indigenous peoples, who have turned to it to address inflammation, arthritis, urinary tract infections, blood purification, menstrual disorders, fever, and asthma.

Modern research is studying this plant for its immune-stimulating properties, which support the treatment of certain types of cancer, viral diseases, Lyme disease, AIDS, and postpartum recovery. In fact, it's a very powerful plant that enhances energy and general well-being, promoting healing and regeneration at a cellular level.

Its Mars-centered essence ignites and supports our system, purifying it so that it can defend itself and restore its boundaries. It also strengthens health, both from a physical and spiritual point of view, letting vitality flow without obstacles or dispersions.

Burning the bark as incense facilitates meditation, enhances psychic abilities, and promotes lucid dreaming; it can also be used in a ritual bath for purification or to remove energetic and emotional blockages. Carrying it as an amulet creates an energy shield, increasing strength and determination.

Let's choose cat's claw for deep purification to clear up intergenerational patterns, freeing and cleaning our essence.

NETTLE

Urtica dioica

Who has never been stung by nettles when walking outdoors? It may be feared and considered a pesky weed, but it's also a bright and nutritious plant, capable of protecting and supporting us like few others.

Native to Europe, Asia, and North Africa, nettle grows in humid places, often near ditches and waterways.

Part of the human diet since the Bronze Age, and known as a cure for arthritis since ancient Egypt, it was widely used by the ancient Greeks as food, medicine, and a textile fiber. It belongs to the so-called tonic herbs, as it's deeply nourishing, and its sting speaks to its ability to reactivate us and stimulate our life force.

It's said that Milarepa, the ancient siddha known for the green color of his hair and skin, only ate nettles. Associated with Thor, the god of thunder with an impetuous power in Norse mythology, it embodies the archetype of the warrior, protecting life by acting on our inner army, the immune system. It's also a plant rich in iron that helps us build and polish our armor against invasion and adverse experiences.

Its medicine is resilience, as it even thrives in poor soils, growing abundantly, spreading and regenerating itself through strong and expanded roots that allow it to emerge like a phoenix from the ashes every time it's uprooted.

It can be used as an amulet, burned for protective magic, sprinkled in the house to ward off malevolent influences, or placed in the room of a sick person to promote healing.

A wise teacher standing firmly rooted in the Earth, nettle does not allow anything unpleasant to influence it, teaching us to set clear boundaries.

Tuesday is a day of action; a time to put ourselves to the test and make the most of our strength by welcoming challenges. We may collect plants associated with Mars; exercise; light a nice fire with blackthorn wood; or cook spicy dishes by incorporating cayenne, garlic, and clove. During the day, sipping an infusion of nettle will give us vigor and lucidity.

MERCURY

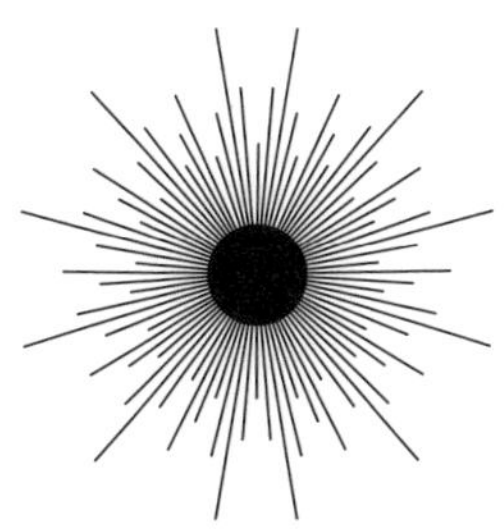

Mercury is the fastest-orbiting planet—and Mercury, the messenger god with winged sandals, is dynamic, quick, communicative, and connected to the elements of air and creativity. Plants associated with Mercury adapt to their environment and often feature mottled leaves and a distinct appearance. They affect breathing, the lymph, and the circulatory and nervous system. They are agents of interchanges with life's vitality.

☿ INDIAN PENNYWORT

Centella asiatica

The shape of its leaves resembles that of a brain. For hundreds of years, it was used in Southeast Asia to hone and expand cognitive function.

Indian pennywort is a perennial herbaceous plant, native to the tropical wetlands of Asia. It is well known in traditional Chinese, Indonesian, and Ayurvedic medicines for its impact on memory and brain functioning.

It has the power to rebalance the adrenal gland, and is widely used as a tonic to strengthen the nervous system. Topically, it improves wound healing and prevents the appearance of scars, properties that have earned it the name Tiger Wort because it's said that injured tigers roll in Indian pennywort to heal themselves.

It's also believed to promote longevity. Herbalist Li Ching-Yuen is said to have lived to be 256 years old thanks to a diet of herbs that included *Centella asiatica*. It's frequently mentioned in ancient Ayurvedic medical texts, and from 1880 onward, it was utilized in Europe as part of pharmaceutical medicine.

Its magical powers relate to its ability to quieten the mind, enhance concentration, and activate the crown chakra. Using it in incense mixtures to be burned prior to meditation helps clear the mind. It's an ally to those wishing to deepen their practice, strengthening their spiritual awareness and dream work.

To incorporate it into our daily lives, we can take it in the form of a nourishing tea, keep it next to us during meditation, fill a sachet to promote dream activity, or burn it like incense to instill clarity.

With its mercurial, fast-paced, and inspired essence, this plant comes to the rescue when we need mental alertness, clarity, and inspiration.

LEMONGRASS

Cymbopogon citratus

This plant is wild and free, growing in grassy bushes up to 3 feet (1 meter) tall, with bright green, drooping, and ribbon-like leaves and an unmistakable zesty citrus scent.

Lemongrass is a perennial herb common in temperate and tropical regions of Eurasia. It is used widely in sauces and soups in Indian and other Asian cooking.

In native areas, it is also called the "fever herb," as it is used to treat colds, fevers, intestinal parasites, and stomach upsets.

Known for its protective qualities, it is also used to ward off bad luck and attract positive vibrations. In the Amazon, it is a popular sedative that is taken like a tea, and also hung in bundles outside the home to repel negative energy. The plant's essential oil is unpleasant to mosquitoes, while its purifying and deodorizing properties are used in cosmetics.

Its lemony scent evokes a feeling of cleanliness that also affects the mental plane, disentangling preconceptions and old patterns and promoting psychic powers. We could think of it like a magic broom capable of sweeping away mental blocks and unbalanced energy, as well as creating a kind of shield against bad actors and adversity.

Lemongrass is a trusted ally in spiritual journeys. Burning it like incense can facilitate spiritual communication, offer a bridge to higher wisdom, and improve clairvoyance. An excellent companion in meditation, it can be utilized in spells and rituals; it's also thought to be one of the fairies' favorite plants.

Lemongrass's energy brings freshness and clear communication, opening up our channels without making us vulnerable.

GINKGO

Ginkgo biloba

With its distinctive bifurcated, fan-shaped leaves that turn golden yellow in autumn and brighten parks and avenues, ginkgo conjures slow growth and regeneration.

Not surprisingly, Darwin called ginkgo a "living fossil," as its origins date back to the Paleozoic era, 250 million years ago. It is the only surviving plant of the *Ginkgoaceae* family and the oldest of the living seeded plants. Originally from China, where it is considered sacred and often found near temples, it has spread all over the world, where it's grown for medicinal purposes and used as an ornamental plant.

It's a greatly resilient tree: some specimens not only survived the Hiroshima bombings but recovered entirely and continue to thrive today.

Since time immemorial, ginkgo has been used as medicine for its benefits to microcirculation, specifically cerebral, proving valuable in treating dementia. It improves memory, instills peace and awareness, and promotes balanced aging.

A cup of ginkgo tea before bed helps recall one's dreams after waking and the development of intuitive skills. It's also a guardian tree that we may approach to confide our troubles and desires.

Ginkgo's gift is that of memory, of being present and knowing how to draw strength from one's experiences and heritage. It's a great sage that knows how to pass through time gracefully and confidently.

HOPS

Humulus lupulus

Famously linked to the production of beer, its medicinal properties were already well known in medieval monasteries, in whose gardens it was always present.

This perennial climbing plant tends to grow over anything in its path by sending new shoots that reach up to 33 feet (10 meters) a year.

Pliny the Elder nicknamed it the "willow-wolf" after noticing how it wrapped itself around willow trees, causing them to shrivel up within a short time. The Latin name *Humulus* comes from *humus*, meaning "soil," on which hops crawl and grow without support. Celtic mythology also associates it with wolves, winter, the underworld, the deity Brigid, and the festival of Imbolc.

Native to the temperate regions of Europe and Asia, hops began to be farmed in the early Middle Ages for its sedative properties and ability to calm the nerves. Because of its anaphrodisiac effect, the church turned a blind eye to beer consumption, as it appeared to help monks maintain their vows of chastity. However, due to the presence of phytoestrogens, it increases the sexual drive in women, alleviates the symptoms of menopause, and helps regulate the menstrual cycle. It resonates with verdant, bright feminine energy and sustains growth and movement, contributing to women's health.

We may keep a small sachet stuffed with dried leaves and flowers under our pillow to promote a peaceful sleep and ward off nightmares. Carry it around in a bag or burn it like incense to promote physical and spiritual healing. Its bitter taste stimulates bile production, enhancing digestion and improving the liver and spleen's energy flow.

Hops resonates with a state of flux, of creative and grounded calm with a lust to grow and expand the heart in the element of air.

HOLY BASIL

Ocimum sanctum

This vibrant green plant, whose lush purple flowers sprout among the leaves like turrets on an enchanted castle, diffuses an exquisite scent that is reminiscent of citrus and licorice.

Known as *tulsi* in Sanskrit, it translates as "the incomparable," while holy basil is also known as *bhutagni* or "destroyer of demons." This herb is believed to be the divine incarnation of Lakshmi, goddess of prosperity, abundance, and fertility. According to Indian lore, the goddess's spiritual powers are steeped into the plant, making it a living blessing. Infused in water, it is sprayed to purify the home and sacred spaces, and it's even used in Greek Orthodox tradition to make holy water and bless the altar.

Placing a holy basil leaf on the chest before going to sleep attracts pleasant dreams and shields from evil. Placed in the mouth of the dying, it is believed to purify the soul and stop the cycle of death and rebirth. The head of the deceased is washed with an infusion of leaves to help them find their way into the kingdom of heaven.

According to Ayurvedic medicine, the plant has a high content of *sattva*, the principle of light, perception, and clarity. Knowing how to instill lightness, warmth, and luster, it increases awareness and helps us open our minds and hearts to love and devotion. It is also said to increase *prana*, the vital breath, and invigorate the respiratory tract.

It is also a highly beneficial adaptogen that supports the body in dealing with stress, protecting the organs and tissues from its negative effects.

All over the world, it is considered a plant associated with holiness. In its essence, steering us toward the sacred and the spiritual, we recognize Mercury's winged energy.

ASPEN

Populus tremula

If we stop and listen in an aspen forest, we might hear the wind whispering through the leaves and murmuring like a gathering of people. That concept is where its scientific name comes from, with "Populus" meaning "people."

This tree, which grows throughout Europe and in some areas of North Africa and Asia, reaches about 82 feet (25 meters) in height and lives up to 100–150 years. The bark is light, and its fronds create an expanse of bright foliage that allows the sun to filter through and the undergrowth to thrive. It's a tree that forms its own tribe, with several specimens growing closely together and favoring moist soil, below which water flows. Thanks to the abundance of leaves that assist in generating a lot of *humus* (soil), the aspen can revitalize arid soils.

The Druids considered the aspen a sacred tree, and in it they saw the expanding of perceptual abilities. They considered it an ally in awakening and nurturing lucidity, clear visions, and clairaudience, as well as connecting with the inner self. Celtic mythology associated the sounds produced by the flickering leaves with inspiration and poetry, as well as the opportunity to communicate with the spiritual world and ancestors.

Christians, on the other hand, branded it as evil exactly because it was a bridge to the invisible. It is said that the Crucifixion took place on a cross of aspen wood and that still today, the tree trembles in shame.

The buds are rich in essential oils and resin, and popular wisdom recommended them to treat fevers, tremors, and paralysis specifically, due to the association with tremors. The bark is also recognized for its fever-reducing properties.

Let us approach this whispering tree to develop the magic of receptivity and cleanse our cosmic antennae, opening ourselves to an expanded and deep feeling of the invisible.

ELM

Ulmus

This majestic tree of the Ulmaceae family is strong and long-lived, as it can live up to 600 years and reach to almost 100 feet (30 meters) in height.

Widespread in Europe, Asia, and North America, the elm is highly appreciated as an ornamental plant as well as for its wood, which is used to make furniture and agricultural tools. It's solitary, growing in the liminal spaces between the fields and the hinterland. Each specimen has its unique shape, a feature that links this tree to Mercury and invites us to express our uniqueness and vocation.

In ancient times, its boiled bark was widely used to prepare medicines to treat wounds, sores, and skin burns. The bark was also used to obtain a cough syrup for colds and sore throats. The custom of making children sleep on a bed of elm leaves was based on the belief that it would strengthen their bones and joints.

Recognizing it as the tree of dreams, clear vision, divination, and prophecy, the ancient Greeks associated it with Oneiros (known as Morpheus among the Romans), son of sleep and night. In medieval times, judges gathered under its branches to issue just sentences. However, in Celtic mythology, elms were associated with the underworld. They had a special affinity with the elves who guarded the burial mounds, the dead, and the passage to the afterlife.

It is a popular tree among green witches, often used in love spells seeking stability and to connect with the divine feminine. Burning a small bundle of elm twigs helps protect oneself from gossip and evil deeds.

Let's choose elm to guide us in recognizing our unique value and gifts, humbly putting them to the service of others with our ancestors' support.

☿ GREAT MULLEIN

Verbascum thapsus

This plant's tall and sturdy stems with spikes of bright yellow flowers are staples that imbue the landscape with a sense of solidity and warmth.

The plant is native to Europe and Asia, widespread in fallow land, and along paths and the side of the road.

Its scientific name comes from the root *virb*, which means "rod," and from the Greek *phlómos*, meaning "flame," because in ancient times, its rolled leaves were used as wicks for oil lamps, while the dried stems dipped in fat served as torches.

In ancient Greece, great mullein was revered as a gift from the gods. Mercury, the messenger god, gave it to Odysseus to protect him from Circe's magic, consecrating him as the guardian against the forces of evil. In the Middle Ages, it was hung on doors or burned as incense to protect the home. In ancient Roman times, it was used in funeral rites, symbolizing the light guiding the dead into the afterlife.

From a curative point of view, its abundance of mucilage (a gel-like secretion) makes it a valuable ally to the respiratory tract and intestine, soothing inflammation and protecting tissues. The flowers are particularly effective against asthmatic coughs, spasms, diarrhea, headache, and migraines.

A small sachet filled with its soft and velvety leaves promotes restful sleep devoid of nightmares and nighttime anxieties. To summon courage and ease the fatigue of walking, it can be placed inside the shoes, and if added to a cleansing bath, it dispels negative energy. By virtue of its affinity with Mercury, it improves communication skills and helps the receipt of divine messages during clairvoyance rituals.

Great mullein is a beacon in the dark, a joyful comfort, a guiding and encouraging lantern, and a warm light to return to. It expands our breath and soothes our path out into the world.

Wednesday is a good day for communication and exchanges dedicated to education, business, and socializing, possibly supported by a few drops of lemongrass essential oil. It's the right time to have some hops and great mullein with us and to listen to others, nature, and intuition. Then, open up to dreams with a cup of ginkgo or holy basil.

JUPITER

Jupiter embodies the archetype of the great father, knowledge, trust, and the generational. It represents access to knowledge in order to enjoy life to its fullest; it is linked to conviviality, pleasure, good fortune, and fulfillment. The nature of this planet is expansive, tending to widen and amplify everything it touches. Plants associated with Jupiter regulate the metabolism; relieve pain; and are emollient, anti-inflammatory, invigorating, and cleansing.

♃ GREATER BURDOCK

Arctium lappa

Its presence is expansive, with large green leaves and bright purple flowers resembling those of the thistle, while its sturdy taproot is well anchored to the earth, expressing solidity.

This wild plant, used as food and for medicinal purposes, grows in Asia, North America, and Europe. It's often found in depleted soils, on roadsides, and in fallow fields. Rarely growing in isolation, it prefers to create plant communities that nourish and sustain the life of animals and humans, regenerating the health of the soil surrounding it and healing the land.

Its scientific name derives from *arktos*, which in ancient Greek means "bear," and from the Latin *lappare*, which means "to grasp," recalling the image of a bear's paw.

It is one of the most widely used plants in traditional healing systems around the world. The roots have a purifying action on the blood, invigorating the liver and rebalancing the skin, as well as healing urinary tract infections, rheumatism, and gout.

Greater burdock's purifying and benevolent magic was used by hanging it on stable doors to protect the cattle inside, and it was added to protective amulets to be carried along on a journey.

It's considered a plant linked to health and sexual vigor, specifically male, and it's used in spells related to prosperity, vitality, and virility.

It can be used to make an infusion for bathing, made into a cleanser to wash floors, or incorporated into a protective spell to ward off bad luck and attract good fortune. To make a wish come true, write it on a greater burdock leaf and burn it.

Greater burdock's character dispenses stability and generosity, nourishing our bodies by supporting vitality and enthusiasm. It helps us to be grounded, both in the exterior world and the one within.

HYSSOP

Hyssopus officinalis

During the flowering season, hyssop appears in all its splendor. With indigo flowers gathered in spikes, its wild presence brightens rocky outcrops and rugged, arid places.

This aromatic plant is part of the *Lamiaceae* family, utilized to enhance the flavor of soups, sauces, and herbal liqueurs.

The name's etymology might relate to the Hebrew *ezob* or to the Arabic *azzof*, which mean "sacred plant"; in fact, it's one of the oldest ceremonial herbs. It's recognized by many traditions for its purifying and esoteric properties. A biblical psalm states: "Purify me with hyssop and I shall be cleansed, wash me and I will be whiter than snow." It's also linked to the Passion of Jesus described in the Gospels.

Hence its widespread use in cleansing incense preparations, for sprinkling homes and fields with holy water, and for making protective crowns to keep lice and—more generally—negativity at bay. In Egypt, priests used hyssop as an ingredient to purify food, while in the Middle Ages, it was burned to disinfect homes, churches, and leper colonies during plague epidemics.

It's a digestive plant that acts as a tonic on the nervous system: its properties are antiseptic, healing, lenitive, and fever-reducing, stimulating the immune system. It can regulate the menstrual cycle; however, taken in high doses, it may be dangerous for pregnancies and must be avoided while breastfeeding.

The infusion can be used for bathing, for washing floors and fixtures, and for purifying spaces and sacred objects. Its essential oil supports the emotional and spiritual cleansing of people and places, bringing together nurturing and a sense of justice.

We seek hyssop's support to make our voices authentic and just, our words sacred and true, and our actions pure and honest.

STAR ANISE

Illicium verum

Well known for its star-shaped, woody husk containing shiny seeds with a sweet and spicy aroma, it is unmistakable, magical, and rich in beneficial properties.

An evergreen tree reaching between 16 and 33 feet (5 and 10 meters) in height, star anise originates from the forests of South China and North Vietnam. It didn't reach Europe until the seventeenth century, but when it did, it was immediately valued.

Its star shape, comprising between eight and twelve pods, has always been a powerful protective symbol. Hung inside the home, carried on one's person, or used in healing rituals, it drives away negative energy and attracts positive energy in connection with prosperity. Its essence is linked to Jupiter, a planet that radiates more energy than it receives from the Sun, master of abundance par excellence.

Burned before going to sleep, it stimulates clairvoyant dreams and wards off nightmares, enhancing psychic powers and helping to reach an altered state of consciousness that facilitates astral travel. The smoke itself can be used in divination.

It is extensively used in Chinese medicine to dispel colds and revitalize and activate digestion. In Ayurvedic medicine, it's used to fight arthritis and rheumatism. As an infusion or an extract, it can act as a diuretic or expectorant, and it soothes sore throats.

The seeds can be kept in a handbag or wallet to attract money or worn as a necklace to entice a new lover or to strengthen an existing bond. When scattered on a bed, the seeds conjure passion and romance.

Let's turn to star anise to nourish our dreams, entrusting them to the stars, certain they'll be nurtured, protected, and cherished until they come true.

OAK

Quercus

Ruler of the woods, the oak is abundant, fertile, and nutritious. With its majesty, it embodies the archetype of the great mother, the great father, and greatness itself.

Consecrated to Zeus, king of all the gods, oak expresses strength and magnificence, wealth and prosperity. Its acorns are symbols of maximum potential, containing all the information needed to generate a new majestic tree.

In ancient times, it was believed that the sound of rain among the oak leaves, along with rumbling thunder, was the voice of the gods imparting messages and omens to priests. The Celts considered oak groves to be sacred, and the root *dereu*—which is linked to multiple meanings, including "acorn," "spear," and "loyalty"—also means "druid," the name of the ancient priests.

Its wood fueled sacred fires, especially in midsummer; acorns provided nourishment to humans and animals alike; and the bark was used as a fever-reducing remedy. Oak galls (abnormal growths on oaks) were used in Roman times and in the Middle Ages to make iron gall ink. The burned leaves are cleansing; acorns can be worn as amulets for prosperity; and the wood can be used to make magical or common objects that express the power of Jupiter in this plant.

Oak invites us to become fulfilled on the material plane, to become participants, and to put our gifts to good use. Just like the acorn, we can express our full potential without becoming materialistic or selfish—simply making ourselves available to the greater good.

Let us entrust ourselves to oak whenever we need support in recognizing our gifts and our power. Let us embrace its majestic trunk as we would a parent who gives us the strength to go out into the world, guided by a broad vision and supported by strong roots.

SAGE

Salvia officinalis

With its spirit of Jupiter, rough silvery-green leaves, and unmistakable fragrance that flavors and enriches many dishes, this is an invigorating plant with many healing properties.

Originating in southern Europe, sage grows anywhere up to an altitude of about 2,600 feet (800 meters) above sea level.

Its name derives from the Latin *salvus*, which means "to save" or "to heal," which references this plant's numerous healing virtues. In fact, it's considered a panacea: the herb embodies the symbol of the wise old man, who has learned from past experiences and has a deep understanding of the world. Its essence lifts the human soul toward an intuitive understanding of nature, of the divine, of life and abundance.

In ancient Egypt, sage was used as a fertility plant, while in the first century AD, the Greek physician Dioscorides recommended its extract to stop bleeding in wounds, disinfect ulcers and sores, and treat sprains and swelling. In love spells, it was used to learn what a future husband looked like. It was also burned for protection to ward off negativity and in rites of passage. Used as incense in sacred rituals, it facilitated mystical connections; the awakening of the sacred inner flame; and ecstatic states, trances, and visions.

It has anti-inflammatory, antidiabetic, and cholesterol-lowering properties; it cures excessive sweating and chronic bronchitis; and it can be helpful in cases of irregular or heavy periods, as well as for soothing the symptoms of menopause.

Sage helps us tap into life's wonder, to integrate its enrichment, to recognize abundance and be joyous. It allows us to ignite and illuminate, shining shamelessly, as the king of the gods—Jupiter himself—teaches.

♃ MAGNOLIA VINE

Schisandra chinensis

A vine plant with a woody stem and fragrant flowers—and recognizable for its shiny red berries—magnolia vine is rich in healing and balancing properties.

The shrub, which prefers humid environments, is native to East Asia and is widespread across Northeast China, Korea, and parts of Russia.

In traditional Chinese medicine, the magnolia vine is renowned for encompassing all five flavors (sweet, bitter, sour, salty, and umami), which correspond to the five elements (wood, fire, earth, metal, and water) and the five organs and viscera (heart, lungs, kidney, liver, and spleen), underscoring how the plant works on a holistic rebalancing of the entire body-mind-spirit system. It teaches us to alchemize polarities, to balance duality, and to go through life with grace, embodying the power to be ourselves and present ourselves as we are. It helps us acquire purpose in life—to integrate profound changes and healing experiences, assimilating the evolutionary stages of the soul in the body.

It has adaptogenic and tonic properties capable of supporting the body in periods of stress and improving mental and cognitive abilities. Like many of the plants associated with Jupiter, it promotes longevity, helping us age healthily and harmoniously, balancing hormones and supporting wellness in an expansive way.

We can drink it as an herbal tea to balance the chakras, purify and strengthen the energetic channels, and balance the rational and intuitive faculties by creating a synergy between our hemispheres. Used as an amulet, it provides deep spiritual nurturing, sustaining us through abundance and in manifesting love.

Magnolia vine is an ally that supports us in establishing and materializing our dreams. It is a plant for inner vision (feminine principle) that is actualized through guidance (masculine principle).

DANDELION

Taraxacum officinale

This is one of the most common plants. In spring, it peppers the meadows in yellow, then fills them with blowballs. Though commonplace, it's a valuable ally for our health and that of ecosystems, and the dandelion embodies the archetype of the selfless healer.

Also known as lion's tooth, it's a purifying, diuretic, and detoxifying plant par excellence. It has the ability to adapt to even the most challenging environments, softening the soil with its large, strong roots and extracting and processing toxins, making nutrients more readily available. The dandelion is a master not only of adaptation but also of knowing how to accept reality by enhancing the available resources so that it thrives in all circumstances.

It brings a medicine of gratitude. It's a plant connected to the liver, the great transformer and administrator of all the blood circulating throughout the body. The Chinese were the first to recognize its power in eliminating toxins and purifying the blood, while the Arabs appreciated its beneficial effects on the liver and kidneys as early as the eleventh century. Knowledge of its nutritional and medicinal qualities spread quickly and has long been recognized widely. It has always been used for the simplest kind of divination: by blowing away the seeds, one looks for answers, tries to predict how long life will be, sends messages to loved ones, and makes wishes.

Dandelion tea is said to improve psychic vision, and, if used as incense, it enhances clairvoyance and psychic abilities.

Its Jupiter-related qualities make dandelion a positive asset for the community, promoting not only the well-being of surrounding plants, including the most delicate ones, but also that of all kinds of animals and insects, to whom it provides sustenance. Thus, it teaches us that shared resources can feed the world.

♃ SMALL-LEAVED LINDEN

Tilia cordata

The enchanting scent that heralds the summer and fills the spirit with the promise of joy gives this tree the ability to speak to the heart and expand it.

This majestic tree, originating from Europe and western Russia, can live several hundreds of years and reach up to about 80 feet (25 meters) in height. Its thick foliage of heart-shaped leaves creates welcoming shade in parks and gardens, while its flowers are much loved by bees, who use them to produce a delicious honey with an intense scent.

The healing virtues of small-leaved linden have been recognized since ancient times. Its origin is linked to the myth of the nymph Philyra, who turned into a linden tree after giving birth to the centaur Chiron, who became an expert in the art of medicine thanks to the teachings of this mother-tree. In Norse mythology, it is associated with Freya, mistress of the Earth, abundance, and destiny.

The Iroquois used its wood to carve totemic masks for healing rituals, while the bark was used for soothsaying by Shiite fortune tellers. In Germanic towns, weddings, festivals, and tribal councils were celebrated under linden trees because they were seen as having a peaceful energy that promoted goodwill.

Planting a linden tree next to the home provides peace and protection, as does using its branches and leaves in the entryway or domestic spaces. In the bedroom, it can make unions longer-lasting. Placing a sachet of flowers and leaves under a pillow will promote rest by fostering dreams and regeneration.

Its healing energy helps to integrate light and shadow. It encourages us to be open to encounters with otherness—to gently embrace that person or parts of ourselves we might reject.

VANILLA

Vanilla planifolia

This fragrant pod, native to Mesoamerica, has a long history linked to pleasure and allure in cooking, magic, and spirituality.

Vanilla is technically an orchid from the genus *Vanilla*, a plant that thrives in tropical wetlands with well-drained soil. It's an evergreen vine that produces flowers only after about two or three years of growth.

Indigenous peoples such as the Totonac and Aztec were the first to harvest its powerful qualities, utilizing it in rituals and healing practices for its sweet taste—and they even used it as a form of currency or tax. In folk medicine, it was often used as an antidepressant and aphrodisiac. Considered the "food of the gods" and linked to creation myths, its scent was believed to have the power to attract blessings and divine assistance.

Once it arrived in Europe, vanilla was immediately recognized for its magical properties. It soon entered medieval grimoires and was often used in talismans, spells, and potions aimed at attracting love, prosperity, and good fortune. Its warm aroma also fascinated alchemists, who began including it in their processes as a catalyst and as an element of personal and spiritual transformation.

A ritual bath with vanilla will strengthen our magnetic power of attraction, while a pod in our pocket can serve as an amulet, inviting favorable energy and helping us face challenging situations more easily by experiencing them as opportunities. Burned like incense, it clears up heaviness and negativity, creating a space for mental clarity and positivity and opening us to abundant visions of ease and happiness.

Vanilla teaches us that gentleness is powerful, evolution can occur with joy and kindness, everything flows better when we relax, and a small effort is more effective than harsh stubbornness.

Thursday is connected to abundance, spirituality, and personal truth. We can devote ourselves to finances and planning, perhaps burning some star anise and sage and following a ritual practice, or making amulets using oak, vanilla, and magnolia. To renew and stabilize our energy, we may cleanse ourselves and the home with an infusion of burdock.

VENUS

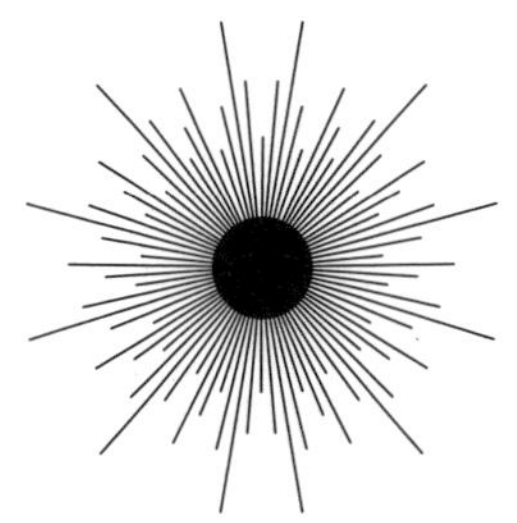

Venus represents beauty and harmony, qualities that complement each other in unions and relationships. Its grace is spiritual, and its splendor is linked to fertile, satisfying health. Plants associated with Venus are soft, harmonious, pleasant to the senses, and nourishing for the environment. They are herbs of happiness, related to the heart—euphoric herbs that boost vitality and invite us to tune in to love.

♀ SILVER BIRCH

Betula

With its slender shape, white trunk, and light and luminous foliage, the silver birch dances to life joyfully, with fluidity and grace.

It's a pioneer plant par excellence as it lives in extreme environmental conditions, making them more favorable for other species. It's even known as the "mother tree" because it was the first one to grow following the end of the Ice Age. In Russia, it's considered the lady of the forest, and in Siberian shamanism, it is associated with the tree of life because the *Amanita muscaria* mushroom, widely used by shamans for its hallucinogenic properties, grows in silver birch forests.

In Norse tradition, the silver birch is associated with Freya, the wild goddess, while in Celtic lore, it was the tree of Brigit, the white virgin who in spring awakens the seeds and announces a new cycle. It's the first of the 22 sacred trees in the *Ogham*, the Celtic tree alphabet. For all these reasons, and because of the purifying properties of its leaves and sap, it's the plant of new beginnings, helping us clear away the old, relax, and prepare our soul and our mindset to confidently begin a new cycle.

In ancient Rome, the silver birch was the tree of Venus, goddess of love and beauty, due to the gracefulness and harmony it emanates—and which it asks us to find in ourselves and the world. Its branches were used to make brooms and objects with a protective purpose, since it is capable of chasing away negativity.

Burning the dried bark of a silver birch is a wonderful way to cleanse a space and create a magical fire in which to let the old go. The bark can also be used to write goals and desires on, so they will be powerful and enduring.

Silver birch's gentle presence and pioneering spirit remind us how beauty and love have the power to change the world.

♀ YLANG YLANG

Cananga odorata

Also called "the flower of flowers," it's distinguished for its sweet and rich floral aroma, taking us to warm, sensual nights in mysterious and exotic countries.

The tree native to tropical Asia, Australia, and the Pacific islands can reach up to almost 100 feet (30 meters) in height and has a thick crown composed of large, tapered, shiny leaves. The lemon-colored flowers are gathered in clusters and are very fragrant.

In the Tagalog language, its name means "wild," evoking the sweet and powerful sensuality of the lush tropical forests from which it comes.

Its origins live in legend, which says that a desperate, childless couple turned to a shaman, who fulfilled their wish of a beautiful daughter on one condition: that she should never fall in love or be touched by a man. But in growing up, the girl fell in love with a man. When he touched her hand, she turned into a fragrant ylang ylang tree.

In Indonesia and Polynesian culture, this plant is recognized for its aphrodisiac properties, so much so that the petals are scattered on the beds of newlyweds to inspire love and sensuality. Its aroma promotes harmony between the masculine and the feminine, within and without—bringing peace, calm, self-love, trust, and the openness required for an authentic and deep encounter with the self and with others.

Traditional medicinal uses include the treatment of asthma, gout, rheumatism, and malaria; it's even used to keep insects away. Ylang ylang is widely used in cosmetics as an oil regulator and to keep hair shiny and healthy.

Yland ylang is a plant that speaks to our senses, intoxicating them and showing us how sensuality and romanticism can make us feel connected to the beauty of the universe.

♀ WITCH-HAZEL

Hamamelis virginiana

When the last leaf falls in the autumn forest, witch-hazel's bare branches spark an explosion of yellow flowers, radiating warmth and prosperity.

This small tree of the undergrowth, native to North America, is widespread in both evergreen and deciduous forests.

Its scientific name means "plant that bears flowers and fruits together," referring to its peculiarity of producing new flowers when the previous year's fruit is still hanging from the bare branches.

It has always been appreciated by native peoples for its medicinal properties: decoctions and liniments were prepared with leaves and twigs; the bark, rich in tannins, provided astringent and healing poultices to be used directly on boils, wounds, and burns; and its flexible wood was used for bow-making. The Iroquois made tea with its leaves (sweetened with maple syrup) to treat intestinal inflammation. In the nineteenth century, the distillate obtained from the leaves was used by European settlers against the sunburn and eye irritation caused by prolonged sun exposure.

The smoke released from burning witch-hazel is said to heighten psychic and clairvoyant skills, providing a clear channel to the spiritual realm and enhancing intuition. Furthermore, its powers are believed to dissipate negativity and offer protection.

Traditionally, its wood was used for the dowsing rods that would locate underground springs, mineral deposits, gold and silver, salt, and other buried treasures.

Let's turn to witch-hazel to find hidden things or lost paths. Its energy of Venus teaches us that even when everything else is receding, neither cold nor darkness can prevent our warmth and our wild inner light from shining.

♀ MOTHERWORT

Leonurus cardiaca

This precious herb symbolizes protection, love, and fertility, and is often associated with the archetype of the mother, who embodies nurturing and protective energies.

Belonging to the mint family, motherwort is an herb that's native to Asia and nowadays grows in almost all temperate climates. Its scientific name comes from the plant's resemblance to a lion's tail and its association with the heart.

In fact, motherwort was appreciated by the ancient Greeks for its beneficial properties on the cardiovascular system, and in the Middle Ages, it was used to ward off insomnia, anxiety, and the symptoms of menopause, specifically to abate hot flashes. Its relaxing action on the muscles makes it valuable in relieving tachycardia, palpitations, heart disease, and menstrual cramps, while also supporting hormonal balance. It's a plant connected to the energy of Venus because it embodies calm, relaxation, and healing, and because it has an affinity with the female organs.

In some traditions, motherwort is used to bless and protect loved ones, and as such is kept with the family photos. Its benevolent, loving, and maternal nature makes it an effective, protective herb for pregnancy and childbirth.

Burned as incense or used in herbal baths, it can cleanse and protect the energy field and help us nurture a feeling of peace and grounding during meditation or spiritual work. On a magical level, it boosts confidence, vitality, optimism, and forgiveness, and it improves intuition and connection with the inner self.

Motherwort is a plant that fills one with courage and soothes inner wounds, taking care not only of the physical heart but also of the emotional and spiritual heart.

♀ LEMON BALM

Melissa officinalis

With its fresh, sweet, citrusy aroma that has both an invigorating and a calming effect, lemon balm is a valuable herb that speaks to inner balance.

This perennial herbaceous plant grows in Europe, North America, and Asia. In ancient Greek, its scientific name means "she who makes honey." In fact, according to Greek mythology, Melissa was a nymph who could transform into a bee and who, at a time when humans were still primitive, introduced them to honey, herbs, and berries. Melissa and the other nymphs fed little Zeus honey, thus giving him strength and power. Bees are irresistibly attracted to this plant, which represents a vital source of nutrition for them and thus is often planted for the purpose of attracting them.

Paracelsus claimed that this herb could completely revitalize the body, describing it as an elixir of life. Sacred to the goddess Diana, it was used in her temples, where it was also called "delight of the heart." It can dispel melancholy, strengthen memory, calm the nervous system, and remove tensions from the body, curing migraines and neuralgia.

In ancient times, it was planted outside the entrance of the home to drive away evil spirits, and nowadays it's a valuable ally if drunk as an infusion, as it can soothe emotional upsets after a relationship has ended.

It can be used in a ritual bath to be shared with a partner, to access divine love and the energy of Venus and to be even more attractive and romantic. With its dried leaves, we can create amulets to attract healing and love, or make herbal sachets to promote relaxation and deep sleep.

Let's choose it as an ally to dispel pain and anxiety; its fresh, kind, and compassionate spirit will lead us to calm and harmony.

♀ POMEGRANATE

Punicum granatum

Its fruits, laden with brilliant red grains, bring an explosion of sweetness at the height of winter and symbolize the dance between death and its opposite, life, in the form of rebirth and fertility.

Pomegranate's reputation spans the boundaries of time and space, stretching from Greek myths to the legends of India, China, and Egypt, as well as finding a prominent place in Judeo-Christian and Islamic scriptures.

The Egyptians used to eat the fruit during funeral ceremonies, as it signified nourishment for the dead. They would make wine out of the fermented seeds and used the bark as a way to keep parasites away. In the Jewish tradition, it's a symbol of justice because its purported 613 seeds correspond to the 613 instructions of the Torah. In China, the grains are consumed by the bride and groom on their wedding night as a good omen for the marriage. It lent its name to the city of Granada in Spain, and it is featured on the coats of arms of many Turkish cities.

However, it's the Greek myths that link the pomegranate to the ancient binary of death and life, specifically that of Persephone, queen of the Underworld and daughter of Demeter (goddess of nature and harvest). Having eaten the seeds, Persephone descended into the kingdom of Hades, where she was forced to stay for six months a year, reminding us of the cycle of life and the purpose of death in the wheel of the year. Thanks to the power of this fruit, Persephone consolidated the power of her kingdom through her marriage with Hades.

The juice and seeds can be used in love spells, for protection, and to communicate with ancestors. Eating pomegranate seeds while visualizing our purpose can help strengthen our creative potential.

It teaches us to scatter our seeds far and wide, to spread many branches, ensuring we have the conditions required to grow and prosper, offering our fruits.

♀ COCOA TREE

Theobroma cacao

This is a magic plant that touches the heart and epitomizes blood as the symbol of life, death, and regeneration, inviting us to access the mystery and beauty of reality.

Native to the tropical forests of Central and South America, this is an evergreen tree that nowadays grows along the Earth's tropical equatorial belt.

The scientific name *Theobroma*, which derives from Greek and translates as "food of the gods," is linked to its mythological origins. The Mayans considered it a divine gift to help humans connect with the powers that guide our existence, as well as with ancestors. Besides its great nutritional value, cocoa was used as a drink in ceremonial contexts—for example, to unite husband and wife in love during weddings and during funeral rites and sacrifices.

Among the Mayans and the Aztecs, before the advent of money, cocoa beans were traded as currency and symbolized wealth and prosperity. In Mesoamerican mythology, the protector of the cocoa tree was Xochiquetzal, the "beautiful lady of the flowers," goddess of beauty, fertility, relationships, and eroticism, and protector of feminine creativity. It was said that her love and beauty could pacify enemies and heal broken hearts, and as such, she can definitely be considered a manifestation of the energy of Venus.

Today, when used in ceremonial settings, cocoa can guide us into heart-opening experiences, facilitating emotional healing and connection, freeing us from old wounds, and opening us up to compassion for ourselves and others.

A symbol of life and fertility, the cocoa tree is a plant that awakens in us gratitude toward Mother Earth for nourishing, supporting, and guiding us toward prosperity.

THYME

Thymus vulgaris

A small and powerful wild plant, thyme comes to us with an intense, herbaceous, and spicy aroma, which opens the breath and expands our love of life.

Native to southern Europe and the Mediterranean regions, in whose culinary and magical traditions it has been known for thousands of years, its name derives from the Greek *Thymon* and means "to offer incense" or "sacrifice."

In Greek times, it was a symbol of elegance and praise, while the Romans associated it with the goddess Venus and her virtues of grace, harmony, and beauty. It's a plant connected to Venus precisely because of its healing properties related to the feminine. In the medicine of ancient Rome, sleeping on sprigs of thyme and inhaling its aroma was thought to cure epilepsy, and it was used as an abortifacient plant. Mixed with honey, in ancient times it was a remedy for respiratory diseases.

The ancient Egyptians employed thyme in the embalming process, and until the Middle Ages, it continued to be burned as incense at funerals and placed in coffins for its antiseptic and purifying properties. It's believed to have been one of the aromatic herbs that filled the manger in which baby Jesus lay, hence its strong spiritual value throughout the Mediterranean.

In magic, thyme is associated with courage, purification, luck, and protection. It can be burned or worn to stimulate inner strength, added to a bath to give clarity and lighten the electromagnetic field, or hung next to the door of the house to ward off negative energy.

Let's choose thyme to ground ourselves in our personal strength, protect what we love, and open ourselves to abundance and luck and beauty within and around us.

DAMIANA

Turnera diffusa

This herbaceous shrub thrives in undergrowth and features small yellow flowers with an intense, spicy scent that is stimulating and capable of awakening our vital instincts.

Native to the Americas, damiana's tonic, antidepressant, and nervine properties have been employed since the time of the Mayan and Aztec civilizations.

Damiana is first mentioned in 1699, in the chronicles of Spanish missionary Juan María de Salvatierra. After that point, its notoriety spread throughout Europe, specifically as an aphrodisiac capable of restoring the sexual drive and reproductive systems of both males and females.

Traditionally, damiana was made into an aromatic liqueur by letting it infuse in rum for two weeks, along with spices such as vanilla, cinnamon, allspice berries, and honey.

It's a plant capable of fully restoring our vitality, and it's excellent for anxiety sufferers. When excessive fatigue results in a lowered libido, damiana can be a valuable ally. It can also be used to regulate a painful and irregular menstrual cycle, as it tones the uterus by increasing blood flow to the pelvic region.

It reminds us that our sensuality is inherently innocent and pure. It can be employed in the tantric practice of sacred sex, or to meditate on the inner mystical marriage: that is, the harmonious masculine and feminine energies in each of us.

Damiana's medicine awakens the body from numbness, depression, and disconnection by expanding the senses to absorb the magic that exists around us. It uses its associations with Venus to whisper to the body that it is safe to open up and experience a healing pleasure.

We pick plants associated with Venus on Fridays and take care of our beauty, relationships, and pleasure; it's a day to be focused on nourishing the senses! Let's start with a cup of cocoa and damiana, then walk among the birches with a loved one. Let's have a massage using ylang ylang or lemon balm, and prepare luxurious and magical food using pomegranate seeds.

SATURN

Evergreen, tall, imperishable trees.
Hard, gnarled plants, growing in hostile environments and speaking to Saturn's ability to value what is essential. Named Cronus by the Greeks, Saturn symbolizes time; its energy is solitary, slow, and ancient. Plants associated with Saturn are meditative and sedative, and encourage recollection. They are also astringent and coagulating.

ARNICA

Arnica montana

This is a resilient and independent plant that reveals its indomitable personality by the way it grows in wild areas, forming isolated, autonomous patches off established paths.

Arnica is widespread in the mountainous regions of Europe and North America, and it grows in poor soils at altitudes between about 1,600 and 8,000 feet (500 and 2,500 meters).

Also called mountain daisy or *Wolfsblume*, it captures the spirit of the wolf as it embodies loyalty, intuition, leadership, and instinct, and also because it is capable of supporting the pack without losing sight of its individuality.

It's a feminine plant linked to intuition and emotional healing that has a long-established traditional use as a healing herb and in spiritual and magic practices. Ancient Nordic stories recount how arnica was planted in the corners of the fields on the summer solstice to ward off evil spirits that could compromise the harvest. It was burned to prevent storms; hung in the house or garden for protection against lightning; and used in spells to attract prosperity, abundance, support, and protection.

Its essence is nurturing and grounding. It's widely used to treat bruises, sprains, menstrual pain, uterine bleeding, heart problems, and much more. Thanks to its ability to stimulate blood flow, it quickly soothes pain and thus promotes tissue regeneration.

This plant should not be ingested, as it will damage the liver. It embodies the strength of Saturn precisely because of its action on the bones and structure, and because it provides support when healing from trauma.

Like a proud and loving she-wolf, arnica knows how to decisively push us toward stepping away from pain and toward health, allowing us to embrace our journey.

♄ SHEPHERD'S PURSE

Capsella bursa-pastoris

Its stem stands adorned by tiny flowers from which infinite heart-shaped pods grow like small purses containing precious seeds.

This essential and earthly plant belongs to the *Cruciferae* family. It blooms all year-round and grows in almost any type of soil, from the sea to the mountains, all over the world (excluding the tropics), regardless of what's going on around it.

It's independent and follows its own path without being distracted. It's abundant and productive, embracing its nature beyond constraints. It aids the Earth in processing pollutants, absorbing heavy metals, and fertilizing the soil; likewise, it helps us process physical and emotional toxins.

In the magic tradition, it's sacred to Frigga, the Norse goddess of love and new beginnings. It was used in protective talismans for healthy pregnancies, as its essence is intimately linked to the protection of seeds (it produces about 4,500 per plant!)—promises for the future.

Shepherd's purse helps us not to scatter and not to be scattered, as it has always been used against bleeding: from nosebleeds to postpartum bleeding, including heavy menstruations. It teaches us to give of ourselves without bleeding out, to rebalance ourselves if we are too constrained and unable to relax, and to keep the life force in our purse for ourselves.

This is a plant that asks us to interrogate ourselves about essence: what seeds are we nurturing through our energy? What is it we want to sprout in our lives?

MYRRH

Commiphora myrra

The shrub from which the precious resin is made is thorny and sturdy, growing in desert areas and embodying life force and determination.

Its origin, as narrated in Ovid's *Metamorphoses*, is linked to the story of Myrrha, a girl, madly in love with her father, who used a subterfuge to have intercourse with him. When she was discovered, pregnant and full of shame, the gods transformed her into a tree whose trunk keeps shedding tears of dense, lenitive resin.

The plant is native to the Arabian Peninsula and Africa. It was already known in ancient Egypt, where it was used in perfumes, anointing oils, pest control, and mummification processes. It was considered sacred to Sekhmet, a fearsome, bloodthirsty deity who had the head of a lioness and the body of a woman, but was also a healer.

The plant appears in numerous ancient texts, including the Torah and the Bible, where it's stated as one of the three gifts the Magi presented to the infant Jesus. It was also used for Jesus' burial.

Myrrh has soothing and regenerating properties on the mucous membranes, and is beneficial for the throat and thyroid. Thanks to its anti-infective and antiviral properties, it's used in traditional Chinese medicine, Ayurveda, and Western herbal medicine.

Its subtle power supports us during important transitions: births, deaths, upheavals, and transformations. It helps us to overcome the fear of separation and feel part of the whole. Its intoxicating and sedative scent leads us into a subtle state of being, contemplating the mystery without the need to decipher it.

Closely linked to the planet Saturn, myrrh supports us in showing seriousness and determination and honoring our commitments. Its magic relates to the tangible, the matter through which the spirit is revealed.

CYPRESS

Cupressus sempervirens

Cypress stands out, pointing straight to the sky with its rooted power, as if it had always been there and was destined to remain there, solid as a mountain, solemn as a monument.

An evergreen belonging to the *Cupressaceae* family, nowadays cypress is found in all temperate regions of the northern hemisphere. It can reach up to about 130 feet (40 meters) in height.

Symbolizing immortality in many cultures, its everlasting presence reminds us of the link between life and death, between heaven and earth. The Greeks trace its origin back to the myth of Apollo and Cyparissus, a young man with whom the god had fallen in love. Cyparissus accidentally killed Apollo's pet deer, his faithful companion. Torn by grief, the young man asked Apollo to kill him, but the god was moved and transformed him into a cypress, a tree symbolizing eternal life and the soul's journey. The tree is sacred to Hades, the lord of the underworld, and was traditionally at the center of the Samhain festival, the Celtic New Year.

Its wood was used to make the sarcophagi of the pharaohs, the coffins of popes, and sacred buildings that could withstand the passage of time.

It is a tree of death and guardian of burial places, but also, in the East, a tree of life symbolizing fertility by virtue of its phallic shape. Its essences are capable of healing. It can be used as a purifying incense; it has protective powers; and it encourages prayer, meditation, and recollection.

Cypress's Saturn-fueled energy elevates us, lifting us out of difficult circumstances, giving us the necessary structure to face change and challenges. Let us seek it out whenever we need to come back to life and ground ourselves to find guidance, integrity, and righteousness.

♄ FIELD HORSETAIL

Equisetum arvense

When we come across it outdoors, along waterways and ditches, let's remember that it is connected to a great and ancient lineage and guided by a primordial power.

Field horsetail, also called common horsetail, descends directly from the imposing trees that grew in the Paleozoic era, between 600 and 250 million years ago. Now it's widespread all over the world, except for Oceania and Antarctica.

This is a living witness to the story of life on Earth, gathering information from a time that is difficult to even imagine, an ancestor whose wisdom results from timeless experience. After nourishing dinosaurs, other animals, and humans since ancient Roman times, it has been used to clean and polish precious metals and stones, specifically weapons and armor, which were said to acquire magical powers this way.

Horsetail is a diuretic and astringent herb that works mainly on the kidneys. According to traditional Chinese medicine, kidneys are connected to our Earlier Heaven—the ancestors and parents who gave us life.

Rich in minerals, specifically silica, field horsetail is an ally for strengthening bones, hair, teeth, and nails, while on a personality level, it helps us work on poise and self-confidence. It can also support us in mending emotional estrangement caused by inflexibility, healing emotional trauma, letting go of grudges, and opening up to the positive, both by drinking it as an herbal tea or wearing it as an amulet inside a cloth sachet.

This ancient teacher advises us to be patient and to have trust when facing life's challenges. It embodies the energy of Saturn, the old ruler of time, asking us to tighten our bond with our ancestors and origins.

BEECH

Fagus sylvatica

When entering a beech forest, we cross the threshold of a wild cathedral, a place of spiritual connection where trees weave deep bonds in a community based on exchanges and mutual support.

The beech is a tree strongly connected to the earth, with roots that wind for several feet on the surface. Its smooth, vigorous, straight trunk, like an imposing column, can easily reach almost 100 feet (30 meters) in height.

Climbing into the foliage with our gaze, we discover that the beech forest is spacious, bright, and airy, open to celestial forces and ready to channel their light. When the sun filters through the fronds, reaching the humid and fragrant soil of the forest, we may witness a great magic: the fusion of spirit and matter, of sacred and wild, and the overcoming of duality through the union of nature.

Walking through a beech forest while meditating is a wonderful experience; it is a pure and harmonious vibration of the forest. Soaking in a bath of beech leaves will help us cleanse and dissolve tightness, strengthening our ability for spiritual connection.

It is emblematic of plants associated with Saturn in how it allows density and structure to emerge. In Celtic and Nordic cultures, the beech was considered a symbol of wisdom, clarity, and knowledge, and priests used it in divination. On the emotional level, it assists in letting go of patterns and rigidity while igniting intuition and new ideas.

Beech is considered the symbol of the cosmic tree that unites heaven, earth, and the underworld, supporting and nurturing the cosmos. It may inspire a feeling of inner freedom that arises from the ability to accept life as it presents itself to us, and welcoming its every aspect.

JUNIPER

Juniperus

Like a green flame blazing across the landscape, Juniper brings purification and regeneration. Its dark, aromatic berries have always been an important source of nutrition during the gloomiest winters.

This evergreen plant belongs to the *Cupressaceae* family, and it can grow in tough environments where few plants manage to survive. It develops slowly, but can live up to 600 years. Depending on the environmental and climatic conditions, it can grow to the size of a small shrub or it can turn into a tree up to about 30 feet (10 meters) high. It's a true healer of the Earth, as it purifies soils and helps repopulate both overcultivated and fallow fields and old gravel pits.

In Mesopotamian mythology, it was a sacred plant linked to Ishtar, the powerful and feared goddess capable of conjuring fertility and destruction; ritual perfumings were celebrated to obtain her benevolence. In ancient Greece, juniper was used as protection from evil spirits and diseases, while the Celts considered it the home of fairies and elves, a refuge for the souls of the dead, and a portal to access the otherworld.

In the Middle Ages, juniper wood and berries were used in purifications to ward off the plague. In Siberia, it was widely used to cleanse and bless magic objects, people, and animals, while in Central Europe, the berries were burned on Walpurgis Night to keep witches away.

Juniper has a purifying action on the liver, kidneys, urinary tract, and joints. It's also used to address acne, eczema, and cellulite by virtue of its antiseptic and astringent properties.

This spirit of Saturn follows its path with determination, helping us do the same. Let's seek it out to cleanse ourselves from any influences, freeing ourselves from limiting patterns to overcome challenges with wisdom and humor.

PINE

Pinus

Uncluttered, long-lived, comfortable in poor soils, evergreen and thus immortal—the pine stretches toward the sky like an antenna that accumulates, then releases, the energy of light into the cosmos with a powerful balancing effect.

A luminous and healing ruler of the mountains, pine's presence is ancient and wise. Like all conifers, it bears a primordial memory, linked to the Earth's evolution. Its origin is rooted in the creative darkness and fertile emptiness that are the realm of Saturn, lord of time. Present on this Earth for about 300 million years, we find it in the elevated mountain forests of the northern hemisphere's temperate zones.

Since it was associated with the god Pan—forest dweller, lover of the wild, and a fertile and protective presence—Christian religion endeavored to eliminate the sacred pine forests to eradicate all ancient cults. The Celts used pine in bonfires during the winter solstice to celebrate the rebirth of the infant Sun, while Northern peoples decorated the pine trees with lights and small gifts, a ritual linked to the more recent tradition of the Christmas tree.

It's a plant linked to inner warmth, to spiritual presence, and to the light that shines within us, capable of guiding us toward harmony with the whole. It's a guide that allows us to understand duality as complementarity and a communion, rather than as opposition. In spirit and matter, masculine and feminine, and light and dark, polarities united in the endless dance of life.

Its soothing resin and needles, burned like incense, purify and lighten the physical and mental space, bringing expansion and evolution.

Pine is a wise, loving, and honorable father who knows how to inspire with his light. He helps us expand our perspective, perceiving the evolutionary design even in the darkest moment.

Saturday is dedicated to discipline, practicality, responsibility, and organization. It's a day suitable for fasting and purification, which we can support with the help of an infusion of horsetail or juniper. Let us be inspired by large trees, stand in contemplation in a beech forest, next to a pine or a cypress; let's create a quiet meditation space by burning myrrh.

ANASTASIA MOSTACCI

Anastasia Mostacci has cultivated a great interest in visible and invisible connections since she was a child. She has studied philosophy and yoga, while at the same time dedicating herself to the study of plants—learning to recognize them, listening to their subtle voices, eating them, and extracting remedies. Since 2015, she has curated projects and initiatives aimed at promoting communication between humans and nature. Accompanied by the plant spirits, she leads evolutionary paths focused on the knowledge and the relationship with the green world.

QUORR

Quorr is a creative studio specializing in illustration, screen printing, and design, mostly inspired by the wild beauty of nature. Founded by Emil Valentini, Quorr is situated in the Dolomites, but is at home wherever the stars can be seen.